1997

Hong Kong's Struggle for Selfhood

Kwok Nai-wang

DAGA PRESS HONGKONG

Published March 1996

DAGA Press
Documentation for Action Groups in Asia (DAGA)
CCA Center
96 Second District
Pak Tin Village
Mei Tin Road
Shatin, New Territories
Hong Kong

ISBN 962-7250-19-8

Table of Contents

FOREWORD

On July 1, 1997, Hong Kong will enter a new era in its history; for after more than 150 years of colonialism, Hong Kong will no longer be a British Crown Colony but will become a Special Administrative Region (SAR) of the People's Republic of China (PRC). This book is an attempt to bring greater understanding of this community's journey in this process. Through this publication, the author, the Rev. Kwok Nai-wang, director of the Hong Kong Christian Institute (HKCI), presents us with the perspective of the major actors in this political drama - the governments of China and Britain - and the implications that the change of sovereignty has on different spheres of life in Hong Kong. Interwoven among these pages, however, is the desire of the people of Hong Kong to chart their own future, to determine what is best for them themselves, to seek communal selfhood. This has not been an easy task though as both the present and future sovereign governments of Hong Kong have sought to deny the sovereignty of Hong Kong's people.

In addition to interpreting Hong Kong's transition from being a British colony to being a Chinese SAR, Kwok also describes the life of the community's grassroots people in one of Asia's original Newly Industrialized Countries or NICs and illuminates the false promise of greater wealth for all if one achieves NIChood. His message is that more wealth is created but that it is unevenly and unfairly distributed. This experience is especially important to share with other Asians as most countries in the region are racing to achieve NIC status as quickly as possible and to embrace its ideology of accumulating wealth through rapid export-oriented industrialization.

We at Documentation for Action Groups in Asia (DAGA) want to thank Kwok for his time and energy in producing this book and for stimulating the people of Hong Kong to participate in their own destiny through his work at HKCI. His vision provides other possibilities and another future for the people of Hong Kong.

Lastly, we at DAGA hope that this book will stimulate awareness about the 1997 issue in Hong Kong, an issue that has presently received relatively little attention on the agenda of activists inside as well as outside of Asia; for as the last chapter of this book explains, both those in Hong Kong and those abroad who cherish the self-determination of people have a role to play in ensuring that Hong Kong's initial steps toward selfhood are sustained.

Bruce Van Voorhis
Editor
March 1996
Hong Kong

Preface

The general attitude of people living overseas is that Hong Kong is affluent; it can take care of itself. They realize that there may be a few radical changes as 1997 approaches; but at the same time, they think that basically the concerns of Hong Kong's people have all been addressed by the agreement signed between Britain and China in December 1984.

The purpose of this book is to bring a deeper understanding of the 1997 issue in Hong Kong, to state that the future of Hong Kong is far from being satisfactorily secured. In fact, there are a number of acute problems which Hong Kong now faces. Some of these are internal problems while others are due to the fact that neither China nor Britain have honored their pledge to safeguard the interests of Hong Kong's people. In fact, both sovereign states have both broken the Joint Declaration regarding the future of Hong Kong, an agreement which they solemnly signed and tabled at the United Nations in 1984.

This book should be seen as a sequel to two other publications in which I attempted to bring some clarity to this topic: *Hong Kong 1997: A Christian Perspective* published by the urban rural mission desk of the Christian Conference of Asia (CCA-URM) in December 1991 and *Hong Kong Braves 1997* produced by the Hong Kong Christian Institute (HKCI) in February 1994.

This current project took six months to complete, from planning and writing to editing and printing. I am grateful for the assistance of Brenda Tam of HKCI, who typed my manuscript on the computer, and to Bruce Van Voorhis of Documentation for Action Groups in Asia (DAGA), who did the editing and proof-reading.

I hope that after finishing this book the reader will appreciate the problems which people in Hong Kong will have to confront in the next several years. I covet your support and solidarity with the people of Hong Kong.

Kwok Nai-wang
October 1995
Hong Kong

1 THE ECONOMY

AN ECONOMIC MIRACLE UNJUSTLY DIVIDED

FROM ENTREPOT TO INDUSTRIALIZATION

Ancient artifacts which have been unearthed in the last 50 years indicate that for at least 5,000 years there were settlements and human activities by Chinese farmers and fishermen in many parts of Kowloon and the New Territories.

In 1841, Britain defeated China in the first infamous Opium War. As a result, Hong Kong Island was ceded to Britain in perpetuity in the Treaty of Nanjing in 1842, and the following year Britain officially established the colony of Hong Kong.

China was again defeated by Britain in 1858. The Kowloon Peninsula (south of present-day Boundary Street) and Stonecutter Island were ceded to Britain under the Convention of Beijing in 1860. In 1898, in the second Beijing Convention, Britain forced China to lease the New Territories (south of the Shenzhen River) and 235 islands to it for 99 years. Together with Hong Kong Island and Kowloon, they formed the entire territory of the British Crown Colony of Hong Kong.

With an extremely well-protected harbor, Hong Kong rose from a group of small farming and fishing villages in the 1850s to one of the most important ports in Southeast Asia in the 1930s. Goods came to China from the United States, Europe and many Southeast Asian countries via Hong Kong and vice versa. Hong Kong's entrepot activities attracted many Chinese people from the mainland to migrate. In 1861, there were less than

100,000 residents in the territory; but in 1939, just prior to the outbreak of World War II, Hong Kong's population had jumped to one million.

As Hong Kong tried to reconstruct itself after its massive destruction prior to and during the Japanese occupation (December 1941 to August 1945), the civil war in the mainland broke out between the Communists and the Nationalists. Thousands of refugees from the mainland came to Hong Kong daily between 1949 and 1950.

Soon the Korean War broke out. The United Nations resolved in 1951 to impose a total trade embargo on China, and consequently, Hong Kong's entrepot functions were severely damaged overnight. Moreover, using the pretext of trying to contain the expansion of "communism," the United States led a military build-up in Japan, south Korea, Taiwan, the Philippines and Thailand. The encirclement of communist China created an extremely tense atmosphere in the region and made the livelihood of Hong Kong's people, which had increased to two million by 1952, extremely difficult.

When Hong Kong was forced to turn to itself, the only way forward was to industrialize. Because of the technologies brought by several families from Shanghai, Hong Kong plunged into the textile industry. In the beginning, it was cotton textiles, gradually woolens and artificial fibers. Even today textile and garment manufacturing form the backbone of Hong Kong's industrial sector. Other major industries introduced in Hong Kong were plastic goods and ship-breaking in the 1960s, which were replaced to some degree by electronic products, clocks and watches in the 1970s.

A Service-Based Economy

After Deng Xiaoping introduced China's open door policies in 1979, Hong Kong's business people turned their attention to the mainland. First, Hong Kong's business community responded fervently to China's many and diversified needs caused by its ambitious programs to modernize its economy, technology base, agricultural sector and military. Hong Kong undertook the role of serving as a supply base for China, especially in the crucial areas of finance and commerce.

Second, because of the increasingly exorbitant cost of land and labor in Hong Kong, its shrewd industrialists decided to move their factories north of the Shenzhen River. Reportedly, more than three million factory jobs have been created for mainlanders in the cities and towns around the Pearl River Delta alone.

Thus, Hong Kong has transformed its economy several times in the past 40 years, from an entrepot to a light industrial center to a commercial and financial center, leading to Hong Kong's service-based economy today. Indeed, Hong Kong is now one of the most important financial as well as commercial centers in the world. It has the world's seventh largest stock market (in terms of daily trading volume); and according to a recent report of *Asia Week*, Hong Kong's total exports for the past 12 months were US$150 billion, which is the world's eighth highest.

The economic success in Hong Kong in the past 20 years has been amazing. *Fortune* magazine voted Hong Kong as the world's most friendly business center in 1994, and the World Economic Forum in a recent report has named Hong Kong the third most competitive business center in the world, just behind the United States and Singapore. In its three most important subcategories, the World Economic Forum placed Hong Kong second in government, third in domestic economic strength and third in internationalization.

In recent years, Hong Kong has enjoyed a healthy 5.5 percent growth rate in gross domestic product (GDP). *Asia Week* in its issue of Feb. 2, 1996, reported that Hong Kong has overtaken

Japan and Germany in per capita GDP (purchasing power parity) with a figure of US$22,527 for Hong Kong, US$21,328 for Japan and US$20,165 for Germany. *Fortune* also named two property tycoons in Hong Kong, Li Shui-kee and Li Ka-shing, among the 10 richest businessmen in the world!

Reasons for Success

What are the contributing factors towards Hong Kong's economic success, from a refugee center in the 1950s to one of the world's most important financial and commercial centers in the 1990s?

First, it has to do with its human resources. Chinese people are extremely hard working, intelligent and easily adapt to a new environment. It is true that a lot of Chinese people from the mainland have used Hong Kong as a stepping stone to live overseas, in North America and Australia in particular. However, it is equally true that a number of people have decided to stay and make Hong Kong their home. This is especially so with those from mainland families who were born locally. Furthermore, Hong Kong has always been blessed with new immigrants from China. They do not mind doing all kinds of manual or even dirty jobs which local residents do not want to do. Hong Kong now accepts 150 legal immigrants from China daily. In addition, the quota for the general importation of labor scheme stands at 25,000. There are also 123,000 Filipinas as well as 25,000 women from Indonesia, Thailand, India, Sri Lanka, Nepal and other parts of Asia working as domestic helpers. We must never forget their significant contribution towards the rapid economic growth of Hong Kong. Thus, while we should acknowledge the contributions made by the entrepreneurs in the territory, we should never overlook the fact that, without the sweat and blood of its laborers, Hong Kong would never have come this far.

Second, a British administrative system, which has included an efficient civil service and an independent judiciary, was introduced in Hong Kong at its colonial inception. This has been complemented by the spirit of the rule of law which prevails in the hearts of all citizens, from the governor down to the people on the street.

Third, since the turn of the century, the Hong Kong government has auspiciously adopted a "*laissez-faire*" economic policy. This so-called non-interventionist policy has helped to bring forth the dynamic power generated by the private sector, make entrepreneurism work, encourage initiatives among all citizens and reward success handsomely. As the governor proudly pointed out in a British Chamber of Commerce conference in September 1995, Hong Kong is the world's freest economy!

Fourth, there is the China factor. Much discussion has centered on how Hong Kong has assisted the economic development of China, but it is often forgotten that China has helped Hong Kong as well. Over the long century, China has provided Hong Kong with cheap labor, cheap food, fresh water, daily necessities and the raw materials which Hong Kong needs. As a commercial center, Hong Kong greatly benefits by having China as its hinterland. The manufactured goods which China exports through Hong Kong and the overseas products which are shipped to China through Hong Kong definitely have helped bring forth the prosperity which Hong Kong now enjoys. In a word, Hong Kong has benefited by being adjacent to China, the world's biggest potential market as well as one of its largest economies.

Many have worried that as China further develops Hong Kong will lose its advantage of being an invaluable outpost to China. Many have even predicted that Shanghai or Guangzhou will overtake Hong Kong in importance as a commercial or financial center on the Pacific Rim, but the fact is that all Chinese cities are still quite far behind Hong Kong in attaining its stature as an international city. Hong Kong now has one of the most sophisticated telecommunications systems in the world. This aids Hong Kong immensely in being a leading global financial and commercial center. Moreover, when further developed, China will need Hong Kong even more in addition to its own ports, like Shanghai and Guangzhou, in order to cope with its huge volume of foreign trade. In a few years, Shanghai may overtake Hong Kong in its importance as an entrepot along the Chinese coast, but Shanghai must develop much more in order to be able to replace Hong Kong in its provision of financial services to the entire country.

Future Problems

Hong Kong faces two major radical changes: one is derived from being an economy founded on manufacturing to being a service-based economy, and the other stems from being a British Crown Colony to becoming a Special Administrative Region (SAR) of the People's Republic of China (PRC). These changes present Hong Kong's 6.3 million citizens with unprecedented challenges. First, they have to adjust to China, a very different type of sovereignty than Britain's. Many have little confidence in the mainland partly because of China's poor human rights record and partly because the Chinese government does things very differently than the British, who, for instance, treasure "rationality"; they often do things according to rules and regulations. The Chinese, on the other hand, value human relationships or *guanxi*. If this kind of difference is not resolved, the unprecedented confidence crisis in Hong Kong may become a destabilizing factor in the community. Of course, optimists still maintain that when there are changes there are also opportunities. That is exactly what the Chinese character for the word *crisis* means.

However, there is another cause of imminent social instability in the territory; for although Hong Kong is a fairly well-developed and affluent city, at least by Asian standards, the wealth which Hong Kong has generated in the past three decades is highly concentrated. For example, the *Hong Kong Economic Journal* on Jan. 2, 1996, reported that the 10 richest families in

Hong Kong possess 51 percent of the shares on the local stock exchange, which had a total value of US$308 billion on Dec. 29, 1995. It is widely believed that 80 percent of the total wealth in Hong Kong belongs to less than 5 percent of the population. Indeed, Hong Kong is a place for the rich and by the rich. There is very little that the middle and lower classes, which comprise 97 percent of the population, can do to check the expansion of this socio-economic imbalance. The rich even concentrate on how to amass more wealth and privileges, and many of the very rich are known to have used illegal means to gain greater affluence. Ronald Li, the former head of the Hong Kong Stock Exchange, and Tsang Hin-chi, a member of the powerful Standing Committee of the National People's Congress (NPC) in China, for example, have all been charged and convicted of accepting bribes or fraud. Many others, like Deacon Chiu, head of a leading Chinese bank in Hong Kong, have also been charged, but proceedings against them were dismissed because of legal loopholes found by their leading lawyers. One senior law enforcement officer said in a recent press conference that it is very difficult to successfully bring those who have committed serious commercial crimes to justice. It is because most of the commercial crimes are highly complex. Moreover, most of the culprits have considerable influence in the territory.

The lower and middle classes in Hong Kong have also been plagued by high inflation in recent years. This is primarily because of the exorbitantly high value of land, a market trend supported by the government. This government policy has enabled the rich to get much richer in the past 10 years. The 10 wealthiest families in Hong Kong are all business tycoons related to property development. The unbelievably high cost of property in recent years has not only made the livelihood of the masses difficult, but it has also driven away multinational corporations, many of which have moved their regional offices to Singapore.

The Hong Kong government and the business community should be worried about Hong Kong's uneven development. In any society, it is always dangerous to base one's lifeline on a single industry or business (in Hong Kong's case only a "service economy"). Hong Kong will be vulnerable if there is an economic decline in the global financial world or if there is a sudden drop in the number of tourists from Taiwan, China and Japan. While the Hong Kong government should continue to initiate policies regarding ways to strengthen Hong Kong's competitiveness in the world's commercial and financial sectors, it must also devise plans to support Hong Kong's manufacturing sector. In short, Hong Kong should embark on a multipronged approach of development rather than emphasizing one sector over another.

The way business on the mainland is conducted should also be a concern for the business community in Hong Kong. In China, it is known that business people have to rely on the officials that they know in closing business deals. The more senior officials one knows in the party or government, the better one's business prospects. This is true regardless of the size of the corporation investing in China or in which country the company is based. The American fast-food chain McDonald's, for instance, signed a contract with the Beijing authorities to lease a shop in Beijing for 15 years. Thus, it proceeded to set up its biggest restaurant in Asia in 1991. Three years later, however, the national authorities decided to move this McDonald's in order to make way for a business tycoon from Hong Kong to redevelop the whole city block where the fast-food restaurant was located. Many pro-China business people argued that they realized there was a problem in China but it would not come to Hong Kong!

Not so, however. In August 1995, Hong Kong-based Cathay Pacific Airways struck a deal with the Taiwan Airways Association. This is a commercial agreement covering air transport between the two areas for a further five-year period (1997-2002). Immediately China disclaimed it and said any agreement straddling 1997 must have China's approval. This, of course, is inconsistent with the Basic Law, Hong Kong's mini-Constitution after 1997, and the Sino-British Joint Declaration that sets the principles under which Hong Kong will be governed under China. Should this be allowed to continue, Hong Kong's status in the international trading community will be harmed.

In the meantime, the whole international business community is watching whether China will honor its promises by allowing Hong Kong genuine autonomy, for it is only when China refrains from interfering in Hong Kong's affairs that the territory's free economy can thrive. Gov. Chris Patten remains optimistic while the chairperson of the British Chamber of Commerce is extremely pessimistic. The best way forward for the international business community is to expose the drawbacks and danger points that they detect in Hong Kong and try their best to reflect them to the respective governments, the Chinese government included.

FEAR OF THE PEOPLE

CHINA'S NATIONAL POLICIES

One of the paramount concerns of China's present leaders is the national goal of "territorial integrity." Since the days of Mao Zedong, no supreme leader in China dares to deviate from this objective. That explains why China cannot abandon its claims of ruling Tibet, why it must try its best to bring Hong Kong, Macau and Taiwan back into the fold.

Since the 1980s, China has made reclaiming sovereignty over Hong Kong, Macau and Taiwan a priority. Macau does not pose a problem, for it is a fairly small Portuguese enclave with only 500,000 residents and an economy driven by tourism and gambling. Moreover, Portugal agreed a long time ago to return Macau to China in 1999. Taiwan and Hong Kong are different, however. Over the past 40 years, a very solid economy has been developed in each area. Since Taiwan is much stronger politically and militarily, China decided to resolve the issue of Hong Kong first. In order to win the hearts of business and community leaders, China decided to adopt a lenient approach. Consequently, Deng Xiaoping introduced the concept of "one country, two systems." According to Deng, when Hong Kong and Taiwan are returned to China, they will not have to relinquish their capitalist economies. Deng hoped that this concept would help soften the resistance of the people in both areas to the communist system.

The "one country, two systems" principle has another important implication as well. China has known for a long time that the communist system is in a state of decay. If it forced such a system on Hong Kong, the city would regress and would lose its economic value to China. After all, China earns about one-third of its foreign exchange from Hong Kong, and the territory is both a vital supply base and a window to the outside world for the mainland. Therefore, China has realized that Hong Kong's stability and prosperity must be preserved at all costs. If Hong Kong continues to do well after it returns to China, it is hoped that Taiwan too may consider rejoining the mainland voluntarily later.

Most of the senior Chinese leaders though have never been exposed to a free economy. They do not understand how a free society works. Moreover, they have been ill-advised by the business leaders in Hong Kong. These people are eager to say things pleasing to the ears of China's leaders, much more so than to communicate to them the realities of Hong Kong society, such as what makes Hong Kong work and what are its problems.

However, the most fundamental problem lies with the fact that "one country, two systems" is a contradiction conceptually and, therefore, is extremely difficult to realize. One senior researcher at the highly prestigious Chinese Academy of Social Sciences in Beijing pointed out that "one country, two systems" is unscientific. It is inherently faulty. Communism in China is no longer an economic ideology (Chinese leaders have accepted the fact that communism has become bankrupt), but rather it is a form of government. In China, the communist government is synonymous with totalitarian rule. As a matter of fact, Communist leaders in China have made sure that this is enshrined in the Constitution of China, which states in unequivocal terms that only the Chinese Communist Party (CCP) is the legitimate ruling party in the country.

The key word for the CCP is *control*. They have to control everything, from the national level to the street level. Chinese leaders believe that there will be chaos if they lose control, that the country will disintegrate if their authority is challenged. That explains why the military, which is fully controlled by the party, was asked to use such excessive force to crush the democratic movement in 1989 as well as all demonstrations in Tibet.

The CCP is exceptionally good at maintaining its dominant position in the country as well through organizational structures and relationships. For instance, at the state level, Premier Li Peng is the head of government, but he has to answer to the general secretary of the party, Jiang Zemin. Similarly, the party secretary in Beijing is above the mayor. In a university, the rector's office and the party secretary's office are side by side. The party secretary makes all of the policy decisions; the rector is primarily responsible for implementing those decisions.

UNITED FRONT TACTICS

In addition to organizational techniques, communist China is famous worldwide for two other things: guerrilla warfare and united front tactics.

A "united front" strategy is widely used by the CCP as a means to make "friends" or to make others think and look at issues in the same way as they do. This is an effective tactic which mobilizes and helps to broaden people's support of the rulers. This works particularly well because in Chinese culture people highly treasure a relationship which is built on respect or "giving face."

In May 1983, China sent two leading party members, Xu Jiatun and Li Chuwen, to head the New China News Agency (NCNA), the *de facto* Chinese consulate in Hong Kong. Li, a former pastor of the International Church in Shanghai and fluent in English, was a highly qualified diplomat. Xu was the former party secretary of Jiangsu Province and a member of the powerful Standing Committee of the National People's Congress (NPC) in China. Within a short while, through hosting numerous dinners, they befriended practically all of the government, business, community and church leaders in Hong Kong. During Xu's tenure, the annual reception on the eve of China's National Day (Oct. 1) was one of the most important social functions in the territory. All of the leading personalities in Hong Kong would attend.

In hindsight, China's efforts to make friends, especially with Hong Kong's business tycoons, has been faulty. First of all, the business tycoons can never reflect the true picture in Hong Kong to China's most prominent leaders. Secondly, business tycoons are all profit-oriented. They want to be close to China's leaders because they believe that these contacts with party and government officials can help them secure lucrative business contracts. Therefore, they are always willing to say things and do things which are pleasing to China's highest officials. These tycoons have no commitment to Hong Kong, and their patriotism to China is questionable. Most have secured overseas passports, and many have diverted their investments overseas.

The price Chinese leaders have to pay by ignoring the masses is that they do not have an accurate view of what is transpiring in Hong Kong, how Hong Kong operates and what makes Hong Kong successful as one of the most vibrant international cities in the world.

The more the Chinese leaders distance themselves from the grassroots, the more they are afraid of them. Likewise, grassroots citizens in Hong Kong are also apprehensive about the intentions of the communist regime. The fact that most of the pro-China candidates have lost in all of the public elections held in Hong Kong in the past 10 years should send a strong signal to China.

From the beginning, China decided to crush all dissenting voices in Hong Kong. China is especially harsh on the democratic leaders in the territory, especially those who try to reflect the general public's negative views of China. Over the years, the mainland has made great efforts to isolate them and even to attack them. For example, on learning that Cheung Ping-leung, the chairman of Meeting Point, a small political party, would join forces with the United Democrats of Hong Kong (UDHK) to form the Democratic Party, the biggest political party in Hong Kong, China stripped Cheung of his appointment as a Hong Kong affairs advisor. Similarly, the head of the Democratic Party, Martin Lee Chu-ming, was refused a permit to enter China to present a paper at Law Asia's biennial convention. Likewise, Cheung Man-kwong, another democratic voice, was not allowed to join a delegation of educators visiting the mainland. In addition, two reporters from the *Apple Daily* owned by Lai Chi-ying, a critic of China, were refused permission to go to Beijing to cover a Preliminary Working Committee (PWC) meeting.

China considers these democratic leaders as arch enemies, perhaps not so much because of their dissenting views, but because they command a large following in Hong Kong and their democratic views are constantly echoed by the international community, such as the world's leading newspapers as well as many governments in the West.

China has never trusted Hong Kong's people. The mainland was especially unhappy about their reaction towards its violent crackdown on the patriotic and democratic movement in China in 1989, which led to the massacre in Tiananmen Square on June 4 and the "white terror" afterwards. On two consecutive Sundays in late May 1989, a million Hong Kong citizens or more - about 20 percent of the city's citizens - took to the streets to express their support for the students in Beijing. Since then, every year on June 4 thousands of Hong Kong's residents still gather to commemorate the violent response of the mainland's leaders in 1989. That explained why in the Basic Law, Hong Kong's mini-Constitution after 1997, which was promulgated in April 1990, China insisted that the following be included:

> "The Hong Kong Special Administrative Region shall enact laws on its own to prohibit any act of treason, secession, sedition, subversion against the central people's government or theft of state secrets, to prohibit foreign political organizations or bodies from conducting political activities in the region and to prohibit political organizations or bodies of the region from establishing ties with foreign political organizations or bodies." (Article 23)

This provision in the Basic Law certainly restricts the people of Hong Kong from expressing themselves freely. It also eliminates foreign governments or international non-governmental organizations (NGOs) from actively participating in Hong Kong's affairs.

THE ELIMINATION OF BRITISH INFLUENCE

China does not trust Britain either. Since 1984, every time Britain has made a decision associated with the territory China has considered it a trick played by London to enhance its own interests or to prolong its influence in Hong Kong. This conspiracy theory has greatly hindered cooperation between China and Britain over key transitional matters related to Hong Kong, such as the extension of bilateral or multinational trade agreements or construction contracts straddling 1997, the localization of hundreds of laws, etc. There are other notable examples regarding the Sino-British feud over Hong Kong as well which are outlined below.

i. In 1984, when Britain decided to withdraw from Hong Kong in 1997, it immediately set before itself the task of creating a fully representative government in Hong Kong. The primary aim as stated in the policy paper, or White Paper, entitled "The Further Development of Representative Government in Hong Kong" published in November 1984 was very clear: "to develop progressively a system of government, the authority for which is firmly rooted in Hong Kong, which is able to represent authoritatively the views of the people of Hong Kong and which is more directly accountable to the people of Hong Kong."

China reacted very strongly to the publication of this White Paper. To China, Britain should return the governing power of the territory to it and not to the people of Hong Kong.

ii. After the events in Beijing and elsewhere in China in June 1989, in order to salvage the unprecedented crisis of confidence among the citizens of Hong Kong, Gov. David Wilson proposed to spend HK$126 billion (US$16.15 billion) on the Port and Airport Development Strategy (PADS), a plan which included the building of a new airport on Chek Lap Kok Island to replace saturated Kai Tak Airport and to improve the port facilities in the territory.

China objected because it believed that Britain wanted to spend all of Hong Kong's reserves before it departed in June 1997.

iii. In 1991, Britain wanted to establish the Court of Final Appeal (CFA) in Hong Kong (presently the Privy Council in London serves as Hong Kong's last court of appeal); but at the insistence of the legal profession in the territory, Britain wanted to allow the court to have the flexibility to invite senior judges from other common law areas to sit on Hong Kong's CFA.

China objected because it felt Britain was trying to internationalize Hong Kong's judicial system. Consequently, China insisted that at least four of the five judges in each sitting of the court must be Hong Kong residents who hold no overseas passport.

iv. The following year Hong Kong granted a consortium headed by Jardines, a British firm, the right to build Container Terminal No. 9.

China again accused Britain of trying to protect Britain's interests in Hong Kong.

v. In October 1992, Gov. Chris Patten proposed to widen the franchise in Hong Kong and to make his own government more accountable to the people of Hong Kong through the Legislative Council (Legco).

China conceived it as the final move by the British to entrench their system in the hearts and minds of Hong Kong's citizens.

Thus, using the pretext that it could no longer work with Chris Patten (who chose not to consult China prior to the publication of his political reform proposals), China sought to dismantle the present system in Hong Kong. Since any system depends heavily on people to operate it, China has decided to totally abandon the political leaders that Britain has nurtured or those who were elected and supported by the people. Instead, China has handpicked its own team of people in Hong Kong.

THE SECOND STOVE

This alternative power base - dubbed the "second stove" by the media - consists of about 800 Beijing appointees: about 20 serve as members in the NPC or the Chinese People's Political Consultative Conference (CPPCC); 30 are PWC members, a working party composed of 57 members whose main concern is to oversee transitional matters in Hong Kong (the other 27 are senior Chinese officials and experts); 100 are Hong Kong affairs advisors; and 670 are Hong Kong district affairs advisors. It is interesting to see who are the citizens of Hong Kong that China trusts.

The first group is comprised of business tycoons. Most of them have built a huge business empire in China and have donated handsomely to China's education and welfare projects. Most of them hold overseas passports. Are they patriotic? Xu Jiatun, the *de facto* Chinese representative in Hong Kong from 1983 to 1990, summed it up nicely in his memoirs. According to Xu, for those in business, being pro-China is a matter of expediency rather than a commitment. A pro-China stance is the only way to ensure business prospects in China as well as in post-1997 Hong Kong. Thus, all sensible business people turn to China, or at least refrain from antagonizing it.

The second group includes retired senior civil servants (one was a former chief secretary and acting governor) and former members of the Executive Council (Exco) and Legco who have lost favor with Gov. Patten and his administration. Their sudden change of allegiance from Britain to China has been shocking. They intimately know the ways in which Hong Kong functions. Now they are eager to offer suggestions to their future masters.

The third group contains the traditional pro-China elements. In a way, these people have more integrity than those in the other two groups; but regardless of their intentions, the majority of Hong Kong's citizens are not receptive to them. This is evident by their near total defeat in both the 1991 and 1995 Legco elections.

Since these 800 people are not elected by the people of Hong Kong but rather are appointed by China, they will not, and cannot, reflect the views of Hong Kong's people. Instead, they will only carry out whatever policies Chinese officials dictate to Hong Kong. This is not to say that they do not have any input. Many of them are only too willing to offer extreme "leftist" views on crucial issues affecting Hong Kong's future. Their intention is clear: they are much too eager to please China's key leaders so that their position and influence will be further consolidated. For example, a retired senior judge suggested that four of the most popular democratic leaders in Hong Kong - Martin Lee Chu-ming, Szeto Wah, Emily Lau Wai-hing and Christine

Loh Kung-wai - should not be allowed to continue to serve in Legco after 1997. Together with another ex-executive councillor-cum-ex-legislative councillor, he also suggested that the Bill of Rights should be repealed and the Public Order Ordinance tightened after 1997 - a step that would discourage Hong Kong's citizens from taking their grievances to the streets, hence, suppressing their criticism of China.

Other suggestions made by the "second stove" have included the following views:

- A provisional legislature should be established in place of the existing Legco on July 1, 1997;
- Legco's Power and Privileges Bill should be scrapped;
- After 1997, Hong Kong's separate and independent status in international organizations should be reviewed;
- Hong Kong should recognize the qualifications of the graduates of more than 500 universities on the mainland;
- Hong Kong's textbooks should be vetted and patriotic education must be strengthened in the schools; and
- The flag of Taiwan must not be flown in public places and Taiwan's president should not be allowed to visit Hong Kong.

To most of Hong Kong's citizens, these recommendations are extremely detrimental to Hong Kong's development. Some of them contravene the Basic Law, and all of them violate the Sino-British Joint Declaration.

THE WAY FORWARD

Nobody disputes the fact that China will resume sovereignty over Hong Kong in July 1997. As the sovereign ruler, China should make a greater effort to win the hearts and minds of the 6.3 million citizens of Hong Kong. Most of all, China should try to project a more positive image of itself to the city's residents.

For example, the NCNA now serves as the official representative of the Chinese government in Hong Kong, but it operates more like a secret society. It does not want to get close to the territory's ordinary citizens. As a rule, it refuses to receive any petitions (most of the petitions actually are directed to either the Chinese government or the NPC). In fact, the guards at the NCNA close the building's iron gate before the petitioners arrive. Instead of this relationship with the community, the NCNA should make itself more transparent. The public in Hong Kong was delighted when, in late 1994, the NCNA organized an open forum to discuss Gov. Patten's annual policy speech.

Regarding who should govern Hong Kong after 1997, China should leave it to Hong Kong's people. This is not only a promise enshrined in the Joint Declaration, but it is also good for Hong Kong and for China. Should China carry out its threat to dismantle Legco, it would have to explain itself not only to the people of Hong Kong but to the international community as well.

There are no grounds for China's fear of the people of Hong Kong and their democratically elected leaders. The people of Hong Kong have proved themselves to be highly rational and pragmatic. The city's democratic leaders do not have a track record of being anti-China; they only wish to point out that China's leaders made a terrible mistake by ordering the People's Liberation Army (PLA) to open fire on the students and by subsequently making massive arrests in June 1989.

China correctly persuaded and supported the participation of the pro-China elements in Hong Kong in the 1994-1995 elections. The people's mandate is the only means to legitimize any government. The results indicated that pro-China candidates had some success in small constituencies but met with almost total failure in larger constituencies. This indicates that China still has much work to do to gain support from the people of Hong Kong.

The eagerness of China to purge Britain's influence in Hong Kong should also be reconsidered. Britain has ruled Hong Kong for 153 years. It has built up a system where there is the rule of law, an independent judiciary, a politically neutral but highly efficient civil service, adequate measures to safeguard individual freedoms, etc. All of these are contributing factors to Hong Kong's success. Thus, China should try to preserve this system and way of life despite the fact that they may be British in nature. For without them, Hong Kong's success will vanish, and consequently, it will adversely affect China.

China should also be more self-confident and pragmatic in its handling of Hong Kong affairs. While it hastens to groom cadres to ensure a tighter grip on Hong Kong after 1997, it must be sensitive to the feelings of Hong Kong's citizens. China cannot ignore the fact that the people of Hong Kong are afraid of the interference of the CCP in Hong Kong. It is no secret that the CCP has been at work in Hong Kong, even before 1949. According to Xu Jiatun, the director of the NCNA serves concurrently as the secretary of the Hong Kong and Macau working committee of the CCP. During his tenure in Hong Kong, Xu said that there were about 600 cadre members under his command. It is advisable for China to review the CCP's involvement in Hong Kong so as to put "Hong Kong people ruling Hong Kong" fully at work. Even one of the local delegates to the NPC, Dorothy Liu Yiu-chu, suggested that the CCP should stop functioning in Hong Kong after 1997.

Finally, in any open society, it is common for the rulers and the ruled to hold different views. Government officials must be prepared to listen to the people they govern and serve and, more importantly, to accept people who hold dissenting views or who are critical of their policies. It is often true that criticism leads to progress. A society is much poorer when people decide to remain silent and dare not express their views openly.

ANOTHER AGENDA

HONG KONG'S FATE IS SEALED

China has always looked upon Britain with great suspicion. The transfer of Hong Kong to Britain in the last century was a sign of British imperialism and aggression against China.

Britain, on the other hand, has always solicited trade with the mainland. Britain highly treasures the Chinese market, which potentially, if not already, is the largest in the world. That explained why in the 1840s Britain used gunboats to force China to open its doors and to snatch Hong Kong, which has one of the world's finest harbors, as a stepping stone to the mainland. Consequently, Britain has no intention of abandoning Hong Kong.

Since 1997 was approaching, at the request of the British business community, Britain decided to send Gov. Murray MacLehose to Beijing in 1979 to inquire about China's views on the matter of Hong Kong's sovereignty. When MacLehose was received by Deng Xiaoping, China's supreme leader, he raised the question regarding Hong Kong's future. Without his aides' prior briefing on the Hong Kong situation, Deng made the following comments: "Investors put your hearts at rest. China will resume sovereignty over Hong Kong no later than 1997." Afterwards it was learned that China was not ready to deal with the issue of Hong Kong's future had Britain not raised it; but to the British, as the lease on the New Territories and 235 islands, which form 80 percent of the land area in Hong Kong, would expire in 1997, some concrete solutions had to be sought in order to enable them to plan their future business operations in Hong Kong.

At the insistence of British Big Business, Prime Minister Margaret Thatcher went to Beijing in 1982 and officially began the negotiations with China about Hong Kong's future. In the beginning, Thatcher, who had just led her country to victory in the military campaign in the Falklands against Argentina, insisted that since the three treaties regarding the lease over Hong Kong were valid all they had to do was ask China to give Britain another lease for the New Territories and the 235 islands for a number of years after 1997. Reportedly, the Chinese leaders were very upset, not so much because Britain had asked for a further lease, but because of Thatcher's strong stance on the legitimacy of the three treaties signed in 1842, 1860 and 1898. To China, all of these agreements were unequal treaties. The Manchu officials were forced to sign by Britain at gunpoint. As a matter of fact, Deng lectured Thatcher over British aggression in Asia. Thatcher was so shaken that she lost her composure and fell on the steps outside the Great Hall of the People in Tiananmen Square after her meeting with Deng.

Consequently, the British had to change their strategy in the negotiations. The next proposal the British sent to Beijing was that Britain would repatriate Hong Kong to the motherland. In return, China would invite Britain to continue to administer Hong Kong for a number of years after 1997. Again, China rejected this idea of "sovereignty in exchange for governing." Finally, after 22 rounds of difficult negotiations, Britain reached an agreement with China over the future of Hong Kong in September 1984. The agreement contained the following important points:

- On July 1, 1997, Hong Kong will be transferred back to China;
- China will allow the Hong Kong system and way of life to continue for 50 years until 2047;

- China will not send an official to rule Hong Kong but will allow Hong Kong people to govern Hong Kong;
- China will give the Special Administrative Region (SAR) of Hong Kong a highly autonomous status; China will only be responsible for Hong Kong's defense and foreign affairs.

In summary, these principles have been distilled into the following phrases: "one country, two systems," "Hong Kong people ruling Hong Kong" through "a highly autonomous government."

APPEASEMENT OF CHINA

Throughout the 1980s, British policy on China was dominated by a group of China experts. Led by Percy Craddock, a former British ambassador to Beijing and Thatcher's special advisor on foreign affairs, and armed with the Solomon Report, which advised foreigners to "give face" to Chinese officials if they wanted to conduct business on the mainland, no British government official dared to stand up to China and challenge the Chinese authorities about their handling of Hong Kong affairs. As a result, Craddock's appeasement or "*kowtowing*" policy greatly harmed Hong Kong's future prospects.

In 1984, for instance, the British government wanted to implement its published policy of introducing direct elections in Hong Kong in the 1988 Legislative Council (Legco) elections; but because of China's vehement objections, it was withdrawn.

Likewise, Beijing objected in 1989 when Hong Kong's people turned out in force to denounce the mainland leaders' crackdown on the democratic movement in China. In response, the British issued an undertaking in the form of a letter from Hong Kong's political advisor in October 1989:

> "The Hong Kong government has no intention of allowing Hong Kong to be used as a base for subversive activities against the People's Republic of China. The NCNA [New

China News Agency] will have noticed the arrest of members of the April 5th action group outside their National Day reception. They will also have noted that the Oct. 10 celebration [the National Day of Nationalist China observed in Taiwan] passed in a low-key way and that the Hong Kong government has recently rejected a proposal for a permanent site for a replica of the statue of democracy [the Goddess of Democracy erected by the students in Tiananmen Square]. . . . The Hong Kong government will continue to have a prudent regard for the special circumstance of Hong Kong and the interests and concerns of the Chinese government."

At the same time, the Hong Kong government wanted to salvage the confidence of the people in the territory. Consequently, during the same month that Hong Kong's political advisor was writing to Beijing, Gov. David Wilson proposed two large projects: the building of a new airport and an overhaul of Hong Kong's infrastructure through the improvement of its port facilities and a new highway system. China objected. Negotiations were pursued. Finally China insisted that Britain sign another undertaking called the "Memorandum of Understanding on the Building of a New Airport and Other Related Matters." British Prime Minister John Major was forced to travel to China to sign this memorandum of understanding or MOU in September 1991 - the first Western leader to go to Beijing since the suppression of dissent in Tiananmen Square more than two years earlier.

These few examples illustrate that, because of Britain's appeasement policy, it has allowed China to renege on its promises to the people of Hong Kong. China has effectively taken away Hong Kong's autonomy. In reality, both governments have broken the agreement bit by bit that they so solemnly signed in 1984. Hong Kong has become a lot poorer for not having the full implementation of this agreement in both letter and spirit.

Patten's Arrival

In late 1991, Major and his Conservative Party won the general election. The following year, because of public pressure in Hong Kong, Britain and North America, the British government called for a change in its policy on China and Hong Kong. Major decided to replace Craddock and Gov. Wilson and to send his trusted colleague and close friend Chris Patten to be the last governor of Hong Kong.

Patten is a British political heavyweight. He was a cabinet minister in both the Thatcher and Major governments, and his last posting was as the chairperson of the ruling party. His presence in Hong Kong was welcome by all except China, which looked at Britain's move with great suspicion.

Patten has primarily sought to do only one thing in Hong Kong before Britain withdraws: to entrench the Hong Kong system in Hong Kong. The way he has chosen to achieve this is to widen the franchise - to allow more citizens to participate in the whole political process - and to make his government more answerable to the people of Hong Kong.

Unfortunately, his plan has not turned out as well as he intended. First, China did not like Patten because, unlike Craddock and company, he did not consult China (meaning to get China's approval and blessing) before he announced his plans. Moreover, Patten went to the Western powers to sell his reform proposals. He was received warmly by the U.S. president and the prime ministers of Canada, Australia and Japan. Consequently, China called Patten a "prostitute," and labeled him "a man of guilt for a thousand years." China even went so far as to stop all high-level contacts with Britain and Hong Kong and promptly refused to support the introduction of the Old Age Pension Scheme, the building of Container Terminal No. 9 and the construction of the strategic sewage disposal system. These measures, thus, forced the business community in Hong Kong to condemn Patten and to accuse him of destroying Hong Kong's prosperity and stability.

Patten has also alienated the people of Hong Kong. They have been disappointed that he did not go far enough in his electoral reforms. In addition, the democratic leaders have turned against him because he has gone back on his pledge to make his government accountable to the legislature. He has also turned a deaf ear to Legco's plea to make the Complaints against Police Office (CAPO) independent from the police force and to establish a central provident fund. Thus, in reality, Patten and his government since mid-1994 have not been supported by China nor by the majority of the people of Hong Kong. Patten's administration, therefore, has become a lame duck.

Dishonorable Withdrawal

Like any other government in the world where Big Business has a great deal of influence on government policies, Britain is no exception. British investments in South China alone amounted to US$10 billion in 1994. The British certainly do not want to have their commercial interests curtailed, for they know only too well how China might react to an unfriendly nation. When the French, for instance, decided to sell a few Mirage jets to Taiwan in 1992, China promptly refused to allow any French firm from having a role in the construction of the underground mass transit system in Guangzhou. The Dutch had met the same fate when they sold two submarines to Taiwan a year earlier. Therefore, in order to protect its interests in China, the British government resorted to its policy of pacifying China again.

In a way, Britain has never put Hong Kong's well-being on its priority list. All it cares about is how to enhance its commercial dealings with China, which explains in part why the British government has rotated the minister responsible for Hong Kong affairs so often. From 1984 to 1995, for example, the following people have served in that capacity: Timothy Renton, Lord Glenarthur, Francis Maude, Lord Caithness, Alastair Goodlad and Jeremy Hanley.

When Britain learned that it had little chance of retaining Hong Kong as a colony, it began to take measures to prevent Hong Kong's people from flooding to the British Isles in the same way Africans did after Britain withdrew from its colonies on that continent in the 1960s. First, in 1981, the British Parliament enacted the Nationality Act that made Hong Kong a British Dependent Territory. Since then, Hong Kong's citizens have been deprived of both the right of abode and the right of entry to the United Kingdom. Of the eight million people who were born in the existing British colonies, only the 3.3 million who were born in Hong Kong have received this kind of treatment. Portugal, however, has treated those who were born in Macau, a Portuguese enclave which will be returned to China in 1999, much differently. Every person who was born in Macau has been given a full Portuguese passport. Since Portugal is a member of the European Union, in theory, all of the 110,000 Macanese who hold a Portuguese passport can choose to live in the United Kingdom but not the people of Hong Kong!

Several years later in 1986 the British government introduced the Hong Kong (British Nationality) Order. The intention of this order was to grant all of the 3.3 million citizens who were born in Hong Kong a British National (Overseas) passport or BNO. BNO is only the name of a passport though. Since then, the nationality of these 3.3 million Hong Kong citizens has been put into serious question. By nationality, they are not Chinese, at least not until after 1997, yet neither are they British. This is a clear indication of how the British have abdicated their legal as well as moral responsibilities towards their citizens in Hong Kong.

There is no indication though that Hong Kong's people want to pursue residency in the United Kingdom even if they were granted full British passports, but many people believe that a full passport (vs. the Hong Kong passport, which is a second-class document) offers them insurance. In the worst-case scenario (which is not likely to happen), they can leave Hong Kong and have a place to go. Even if one day Hong Kong's people would have to go to the United Kingdom, they would only be an asset, not a liability to the country. This has been vindicated in both Canada and Australia.

Hong Kong's people now do not have any illusion about the British government's willingness to take care of them as it has promised. Hong Kong's people feel that at this critical moment in their history they are being abandoned or even betrayed. In return, Britain cannot expect Hong Kong's citizens to stand on its side in any Sino-British feud. Hong Kong's people, especially its democratic leaders, have found it extremely difficult to support the British government because its policies on China and Hong Kong waver all the time. In short, whether Britain confronts China or whether it compromises with China, the welfare of the people of Hong Kong is always overlooked and sacrificed.

In summary, Britain all along wanted to have an honorable withdrawal from Hong Kong. Its plan was to entrench the Hong Kong system and way of life in the community so that these could survive after 1997. To the British, the Hong Kong system and way of life are not only good for the people of Hong Kong but for British traders as well. In this context, the British have undertaken the actions below in the past decade.

i. **Improve Local Infrastructure:** More than HK$200 billion (US$25.6 billion) has been spent to improve the highway system and port facilities, undertake land reclamation and build a new airport on Chek Lap Kok Island, and HK$20 billion (US$2.6 billion) has been allocated to overhaul the strategic sewage disposal system.

ii. **Introduce Adequate Checks and Balances in the Local Administration and Improve Its Efficiency:** The former includes opening up the political process and the latter to privatizing important government services by establishing corresponding authorities, like the Housing Authority and the Hospital Authority. Public car parks and most of the tunnels have also been successfully privatized. In the next two years, urban services, social welfare and perhaps the postal service will follow the same path. However, because of China's objection, the privatization of Radio Television Hong Kong (RTHK) has been postponed.

***iii.* Expand Civil Liberties:** A Bill of Rights was enacted in June 1991, and several draconian laws have been amended.

***iv.* Localize the Civil Service:** Presently, with the exception of the governor and attorney general, the other 18 most senior officials are local people. Regarding more junior officers, the Legal Department and the judiciary are not progressing as well. This is because local barristers and lawyers prefer private practice to service in the government because the former offers more lucrative material rewards.

***v.* Improve the Qualifications and Caliber of the Work Force by Expanding Tertiary Education:** In 1960, there was only one university, and the intake of first-year degree candidates was 350. In 1994, the intake of first-year degree students jumped to 14,500. This represented 17.7 percent of the relevant age group or 50 percent of the students who took the entrance examinations. Together, there are seven degree-granting institutions in Hong Kong today, namely: Hong Kong University, the Chinese University of Hong Kong, the University of Science and Technology, Polytechnic University, the City University of Hong Kong, Baptist University and Lingnan College.

4 LOCAL ADMINISTRATION

GOVERNMENT FOR THE ELITE

EXECUTIVE-LED GOVERNMENT

The Hong Kong government is executive-led. The governor and his 20 senior officials, led by the chief secretary, the financial secretary, the attorney general and 17 branch secretaries, make all important policy decisions. The government's 180,000 civil servants, which belong to about 50 departments, implement these policy decisions faithfully and effectively.

In Hong Kong, the civil service is one of the most important pillars in the community. It is politically neutral, and its efficiency is well-known throughout the world. Although it is generally unchecked, it is relatively honest, especially since the powerful Independent Commission against Corruption (ICAC) was formed in 1974.

Basically, however, the Hong Kong government is highly "elitist." Its senior officials are the best of Hong Kong society. They are highly intelligent with a solid educational background and are well-trained. They are also supported by thousands of "elitists" drawn from all sectors. Every senior official has his or her own advisors; every government department has at least a statutory advisory body.

The civil servants in Hong Kong are also very well-rewarded. A policy secretary, for example, earns HK$157,250 (US$20,160) per month. They all have housing (government quarters are generously large), a chauffeured car, an education allowance for their children, free annual or biannual holidays and good medical and dental care. In fact, the governor of Hong Kong's salary is double that of the British prime minister!

In recent years, however, the stability of the civil service seems to have been disrupted. First of all, as Robert Broadfoot, director of a political and economic risk consultancy firm, put it: "One of the main causes for the unrest is the government's miserly attitude towards the staff."

It is a fact that increasingly the gap between government revenue and staff benefits is widening. In the last five years, this disparity has grown at an average rate of 10 percent per year. Consequently, the only option left for the Hong Kong government is to reduce its expenses as expeditiously as possible. The most drastic measure is to maintain almost zero growth in the entire civil service, or worse still, in some cases, to reduce the number of staff in specific departments. This creates a dilemma in which the same number of staff have to cope with an ever increasing workload.

Secondly, as Nicholas Yeh, the acting deputy secretary for the civil service, once observed: "The civil service is not immune to the uncertainly felt by the community as a whole because of 1997." To be specific, civil servants on the whole are worried about the security of their pensions despite repeated promises by China. The result is that a large number of civil servants have asked for early retirement.

Senior civil servants are also worried about their future prospects. Will China continue to need their services? Reportedly, this is the principal reason why 50 percent of the most senior police officers are not planning to serve beyond 1997. This was also the reason why Michael Sze, the secretary for civil service, decided to leave the government in February 1996. Sze was rebuked by China several times when he served as secretary for constitutional affairs and defended Gov. Chris Patten's constitutional reform proposals between 1992 and 1994. Other senior civil servants have also decided to leave the government and join the private sector as senior executives. There are others too who have resigned in favor of emigration.

This has forced the government to reshuffle its most senior staff members almost once every two months. Lam Woon-kwong, the deputy director of education and manpower, for example, was nominated as the commissioner of labor. Before he began his new job, he was reassigned to be the director of education. After he had worked in this job for less than a year, he was named as the new secretary for civil service. By one estimate, of the top 20 civil servants, the average number of years they have been at their present post is two years. As Sze noted, frequent changes promote instability within the civil service.

The high departure rate of senior civil servants means a loss of invaluable experience in the civil service. The fact-finding report on a landslide in Deep Bay and another on the Tuen Mun highway in August 1995 indicate that government departments lack coordination and individual officials are poor in handling crises.

The large number of senior officials at the highest level who have left the government and joined the private sector should be another cause of concern for the wider community of Hong Kong as well. Undoubtedly, all senior civil servants have access to a great deal of classified data and extremely sensitive information. If they transfer to the private sector with these secrets, their companies certainly will use this vital information to their advantage. This will put Hong Kong's image of a market based on "fair competition" in jeopardy.

Furthermore, in the executive-led government in Hong Kong, these senior officials are responsible for formulating all important decisions affecting the commercial sector. If these officials want a lucrative post in business immediately after they leave the civil service, it is only natural that they have their future employer's interests in mind when they make decisions.

The public trust of the civil service as well as the executive-led government is, thus, at stake. Times have changed. The local administration that has served Hong Kong for more than 150 years has to be thoroughly reviewed.

PRO-BUSINESS POLICIES

The Letters Patent and Royal Instructions (the mini-Constitution of the British Crown Colony in Hong Kong) give the governor of Hong Kong almost unlimited powers to govern the territory. He appoints four senior government officials and about 10 private citizens to constitute the Executive Council (Exco), which meets once a week behind close doors. Traditionally, it is in these meetings that the governor makes all important policy decisions.

Exco though is monopolized by Big Business. Many Exco members are business tycoons. For the few who are not, they also tend to reflect the views of Big Business.

In late 1992, the chief executive of the Hong Kong and Shanghai Bank (the central bank in Hong Kong), William Purves, decided to return to London as the bank had moved its main office there. Many predicted the Exco seat vacated by Purves would be filled by a person who would support Patten. After many months of deliberation, Patten could not resist the lobbying of Big Business and announced that he would appoint Purves' successor, John Gray, to Exco. Gray, however, was an outspoken critic of Patten's political reform proposals. Similarly, another business tycoon, Qian Quo-feng, who challenged Patten's reforms is another Exco member.

In 1968, Richard Hughes, a well-known Australian columnist, wrote a book entitled *Hong Kong: Borrowed Time, Borrowed Place*. In his book, Hughes asserted that the power structure of

Hong Kong was as follows: the Royal Hong Kong Jockey Club (where the most influential business people congregate), Jardine Matheson and Co. (the biggest British firm in Hong Kong from the 1870s to the 1970s), the Hong Kong and Shanghai Banking Corp. and the governor in that order.

In this power structure, the Hong Kong government is extremely pro-business. In spite of measures taken in 1994 to constrain property speculation and the high housing costs it had caused, the government's overall policy has been historically to support high land values that benefit only a very small group of property developers. This policy, which makes both residential and commercial rentals among the highest in the world, affects not only the quality of life of half of the population in Hong Kong but also drives away many multinational corporations. The Japanese department store Mitsukoshi, one of the largest in Hong Kong, for instance, closed its Tsim Sha Tsui branch because of exorbitant rentals in 1995. During the same year, thousands of other shops, restaurants, factories and business firms were shut down as well simply because they could no longer afford to pay the disproportionately high rentals. As a result, Hong Kong lost more than 40,000 jobs.

The Hong Kong government is always proud of informing the outside world that Hong Kong's tax structure is both very simple and very low. In 1993, the Hong Kong government had to use all of its muscle though to push the Hong Kong profits tax back to 17.5 percent, an increase of 1 percent from 1992. Yet even with this modest increase, there is still no comparison to the rates in Asia's other three dragons (27 percent in Taiwan, 31 percent in Singapore and 34 percent in south Korea).

POOR ACCOUNTABILITY

The civil service in Hong Kong is not accountable to the public. Every civil servant is accountable to only his or her supervisor. It is a very closed system. Thus, its accountability is neither open nor independent.

Several years ago, for example, a government-subsidized hospital was sued for negligence because a patient under its care suddenly became incapacitated because of brain damage sustained during an operation. A senior doctor at a government hospital commented later that this kind of tragedy would usually never be known by the public, indicating that it is customary practice for supervisors to conceal from the community any mistakes committed by doctors and staff under their management.

Senior government officials outside of the medical establishment in Hong Kong are extremely poor in assuming responsibility for their errors as well. In 1994 when it was discovered that the noise level at a recently renovated government stadium exceeded the limit permitted by law, causing an uproar, the secretary for culture and recreation said that his branch should not be blamed, making the major donor of the project, the Jockey Club, extremely annoyed. The general public promptly demanded his resignation; but after more than a year, he still remains in his post.

A similar lack of responsibility was assumed by an official in explaining the government's response to an act of Nature; for when a section of the Tuen Mun highway was closed for eight days in 1995 because of the danger of a landslide, the result was chaos for traffic between this community in the New Territories and the rest of the city. In a press conference, instead of being apologetic for the whole episode, an assistant commissioner of transport tried to explain away the problem by saying that it was God's will that there should be so much rain on the weekend and, therefore, the closure had to begin on a Monday when traffic is always congested.

Other acts of denial are related to violence though and, thus, have much more serious implications. In April 1994, 1,200 police and correctional officers were sent to the Whitehead Detention Center to move 1,500 Vietnamese detainees to Sai Kung. Five hundred rounds of tear gas were fired; more than 200 detainees were injured. Afterwards the government inquiry confirmed that excessive force was used. Immediately, however, the police declared that there was not enough evidence to bring criminal charges against any of the officers involved. This was extremely disturbing. Widespread assaults were committed. If the officers were not responsible, who was responsible - the person in charge of the operation - the commissioner of correctional services? The commissioner claimed promptly after the operation though that only minimum force was used. If he was not responsible, was the secretary for security, who must have given his final approval, at fault? Somebody should take administrative responsibility for this operation which caused suffering to so many Vietnamese asylum seekers and the reputation of Hong Kong as an international city. The Hong Kong government fell far below acceptable standards of accountability in this case.

In its relations with the legislature, the question arises of whether officials direct the government or whether the institution of government dictates the response of its policy makers. In Hong Kong, the amendment of existing laws or the introduction of new laws have to be endorsed by the Legislative Council (Legco). For many years, Legco was treated by officials as a rubber stamp. In 1994, the secretary for education and manpower, Leung Man-kin, wanted Legco to pass the Workers' Compensation (Amendment) Bill. He threatened that if Legco further amended his bill he would have no hesitation in withdrawing it. A Legco member, Lau Chin-shek, who is also the director of the Hong Kong Christian Industrial Committee (HKCIC), retorted that if Leung withdrew the bill he would resign. After a long debate, Legco was able to amend Leung's proposal; Leung withdrew the bill; and Lau resigned. This indicated the folly of, not so much the Hong Kong system, but rather the narrow and rigid mindset of government officials.

The Hong Kong government also tightly guards the way in which it actually operates as well as the relevant data and information which support its policy decisions. Practically all government documents are stamped in red with such words as "restricted," "classified," "confidential" or "top secret," and they are not, of course, accessible to the public. Without such information, the public can hardly influence or monitor the government's decisions.

The governor and his deputy, the chief secretary, have argued forcefully since 1992 that Hong Kong must have an open and accountable government. Yet what they have done falls far short of what they have advocated; for in 1994, it was discovered that Gov. Patten had secretly asked the Privy Council in London to amend the Letters Patent so that 20 seats in Legco could be returned by direct election from the geographical constituencies. Yet at the time, the general public and Legco were still debating whether the 20 seats should be increased to 30 or even the entire legislature of 60 seats! If Patten had already made up his mind about the issue, why did he continue to pretend that the matter was still open for public debate and mislead the community into thinking that some degree of democracy existed. Instead, in reality, pseudodemocracy was at work in Hong Kong.

This attitude of secrecy was also evident in the meeting between the chief secretary and the director of the Hong Kong and Macau Affairs Office in Beijing in the middle of 1995. It was the first contact at such a senior level in two years, yet she chose to fly from London to Beijing quietly, and not a word of substance about such an important meeting was disclosed upon her return.

A Time for Change

The world continues to evolve very rapidly and so does Hong Kong. The territory has changed tremendously in the past 20 years. In order to better serve the entire community, the Hong Kong government must be revamped as well.

First, it should allow Legco, the only political structure in the central government of the territory with a public mandate, to take a more active role in assisting it to shape its public policies in Hong Kong.

Since 1991 when the electorate was able to directly cast a ballot for its representatives in Legco for the first time, the legislature has become more assertive. Many outspoken elected councillors have been critical of the way the government has operated. A few have even taken the initiative of introducing private members' bills concerning crucial issues in Hong Kong. The most notable examples have been Christine Loh Kung-wai's Access of Information Bill, Emily Lau Wai-hing's Election Bill (calling for all 60 seats in Legco to be returned by universal franchise) and Anna Wu Hung-yuk's Equal Opportunities Bill and Human Rights Commission Bill. Reportedly, senior government officials have been very annoyed, so much so that they have contemplated crippling Legco by not allowing it to introduce any bills at all. If that should happen, it would be a serious setback for Hong Kong's constitutional development.

It is hoped that Patten, himself an elected politician from Britain, would encourage Legco to be more actively involved in working together with the Hong Kong government. He should take the lead to demonstrate how his government is accountable (meaning answerable and responsive) to the legislature. He should refrain from invoking the Royal Instructions to veto any Legco proposal he dislikes, such as the unanimous decision made by Legco in 1994 to freeze property rates for two years. Since Patten's lieutenants at the time were more interested in maintaining the status of an executive-led government, they persuaded Patten to overrule the will of the legislature.

Secondly, as an open and civilized society, Hong Kong needs a comprehensive Equal Opportunities Bill. This is the only way to outlaw all forms of discrimination. In addition, in order to better safeguard the basic human rights of its people, Hong Kong needs a Human Rights Commission, especially for advocacy and education; and in order to enhance freedom of expression, there should be a public access channel (Cable Television, if the government approves, can provide such a channel with limited administrative costs). For the welfare of the whole community, the Hong Kong government should withstand pressure from China and implement all of these important measures immediately.

Thirdly, the concept that "government is for the people" must be taken more seriously by the Hong Kong government. As the government is for the people (meaning *all* the people it governs), it should resist the temptation of giving special favors to the few who are privileged and wealthy. Entrepreneurs are always profit-oriented. They do not even want to pay an additional 5 percent to support the Old Age Pension Scheme (OAPS). In order to provide all citizens better protection, the government should never have listened to the territory's employers when it rejected the OAPS. After all, the International Covenant on Economic, Social and Cultural Rights (ICESCR) of which Britain is a signatory stipulates that "every citizen has a right to social security" (cf. Article 9).

In addition to serving the community more fairly, the Hong Kong government should also find ways to improve its quality of service. Hong Kong government officials should learn how to respond to issues more professionally. In 1994, the secretary for planning, environment and lands decided to test the waters and briefed selected brokers about his package to curb property prices prior to its release to the public and while the stock market was still trading. It provoked an uproar in the territory. Many asked whether any of the brokers took advantage of the briefing and benefited financially from it. In similar fashion, the financial secretary allowed the Hong Kong Stock Market to close for three days in 1987 in order to avoid the great turbulence which hit the stock markets throughout the world at that time. Investors worldwide were furious. This decision also greatly damaged the reputation of Hong Kong as an international financial center.

By and large, the Hong Kong government needs to improve its long-range planning. Twenty years ago when it decided to build a new town in Tuen Mun and put half-a-million residents there, it failed to foresee the need of a mass transit system to ferry about 300,000 commuters daily to Kowloon or Hong Kong Island. Consequently, whenever there is an accident on the Tuen Mun highway, traffic is almost brought to a standstill. A similar pattern of questionable planning has led to incessant reclamation on both sides of the harbor, and the permission to allow developers to build golf courses and residential blocks on invaluable green belts or even in country parks in the New Territories will certainly destroy Hong Kong's environment. Because of all these dubious decisions, our children will have to live in an unhealthy concrete jungle with highly polluted air, water, noise and waste.

Finally, the Hong Kong government should lay a more solid foundation and set higher standards for the post-1997 Hong Kong Special Administrative Region (SAR) government. We have to consider that after 1997 all secretaries (equivalent to ministers in a national government) and other important posts, like the commissioner of police, the ICAC commissioner, etc., will be appointed by the central government in Beijing. People can and do influence the system they operate. Beijing can, therefore, influence the Hong Kong system and way of life through the people they appoint. That is why Hong Kong must use the remaining 500 days before the transfer of its sovereignty to build mechanisms whereby the executive-led government in Hong Kong can be checked and its policies can be monitored closely by the citizens of Hong Kong or the representatives that they elect.

THE RULE OF LAW OR THE RULE OF GUANXI?

RULE OF LAW RUPTURED BY BOTH SOVEREIGN GOVERNMENTS

The rule of law is one of the most important pillars in any modern society. If motorists do not obey signals and regulations, they will bring city traffic to a standstill. Similarly, if hikers in Hong Kong's country parks do not observe the "light no fire" warning, soon the remaining trees will be gone, and the last vestiges of Nature in Hong Kong will also become a part of its concrete jungle. The rule of law is more important, however, to the business community than to people on the street. It would be extremely bad for business if contracts and agreements were not strictly observed. The rule of law also guarantees fair competition. The rule of law, thus, is a major contributing factor towards Hong Kong's success. The city's economic development would not have been so great in the 1970s and 1980s if the Independent Commission against Corruption (ICAC) had not been founded in 1974. The ICAC has done a tremendous job in ensuring that both the civil service and the private sector act according to the law.

However, as 1997 approaches and as China increases its influence in Hong Kong's affairs, there are numerous signs that the rule of law has begun to erode in the territory.

Unlike Hong Kong, there has never been any tradition of the rule of law on the mainland. In China, people are ruled by those who possess power. Most often the power of contemporary Chinese leaders, as Mao Zedong observed, has come with "the barrel of the gun." In other words, on the mainland, the rule of law is subservient to the rule of party cadres or officials who hold authority. The present Constitution stipulates that the Chinese Communist Party (CCP) is the only legitimate ruling party in the nation. The party is, therefore, above the State. In practice, the party leaders are even above the party itself. Zhao Ziyang, the former party chief, once said that all important decisions regarding the nation or the State should be confirmed by Deng Xiaoping, the supreme leader of the party. Up to this day, this practice remains the same despite the fact that Deng holds no official position in the party, the State or the military!

This is how China functions. Jiang Zemin, the party chief, ranks far above Premier Li Peng. In a city, the mayor is answerable to the city's party boss. In any university, the rector or president is only responsible for the day-to-day administration of the institution. The party secretary, who sits next to the rector's office, makes all of the key policy decisions. Thus, this is the mainland Chinese system in which the party holds absolute power over all final decisions.

In this system of rule by personalities, corruption abounds. Jiang has vowed to put an anti-corruption campaign at the top of his agenda. Indeed, in recent years, many corrupt senior officials have been purged. Chen Xitong, the party secretary of Beijing and a Politburo member, was removed from his post in 1995 and expelled from the CCP because of serious corruption charges against him. It is widely believed though that this is only the beginning. The "princeling" faction - the sons and daughters of party leaders - is thought to be one of the most corrupt networks on the mainland; yet because of their close relationship with the country's most powerful leaders, nobody dares to accuse them of any wrongdoing. In China, "relationship" or "*guanxi*" (literally means "connection") is of the utmost importance. If you are connected with the right person, you can bypass all of the rules and regulations. Oftentimes *guanxi* is bought with expensive gifts or with large amounts of money.

Hong Kong's people are nervous that this Chinese way of achieving results is gradually migrating to Hong Kong as those who represent the party, the State and the military in China are the largest investors in Hong Kong. They are apprehensive because Chinese officials often do things according to their liking rather than to the requirements of the law. According to the Hong Kong government, in the last few years, the Hong Kong Marine Police have recorded and even filmed 80 incursions into Hong Kong's waters by Chinese Public Security Bureau (PSB) gunboats. If they do not respect Hong Kong while it is still under British rule, how much more will they abuse the boundaries of Hong Kong once it becomes a part of Chinese territory?

There is yet another more serious area which Hong Kong's citizens have overlooked, for China, at its whim, is violating the agreements which it has promised Hong Kong it will uphold. This greatly threatens to undermine the rule of law in Hong Kong after 1997.

First, there is concern about the future Court of Final Appeal (CFA). The Privy Council in London now serves in this capacity for Hong Kong. According to the Basic Law, the mini-Constitution of post-1997 Hong Kong, the CFA will be established in Hong Kong before 1997; but after many rounds of negotiations, an agreement was reached between China and Britain in June 1995 that specifies that the CFA will only be established upon the transfer of sovereignty in July 1997. More worrisome, however, are the stipulations that no more than one judge who holds a foreign passport can sit on the five-member panel of judges and that the CFA has no jurisdiction over "acts of state." These restrictions not only greatly limit the functions of the CFA, but they also deviate significantly from the Basic Law. Article 82, for example, states that "the power of final adjudication of the

Hong Kong Special Administrative Region shall be vested in the CFA of the region, which may, as required, invite judges from other common law jurisdictions to sit on the CFA." In other words, according to the Basic Law, it is up to the CFA to decide how many overseas judges it should invite. Thus, this agreement between Hong Kong's present and future sovereign powers not only breaks the law, but it also causes great damage to the judiciary's independence.

The judiciary, however, is not the only branch of government that has been affected by a disregard for prior legal agreements, for China, through a resolution of the National People's Congress (NPC), has decided to dismantle the existing Legislative Council (Legco) in Hong Kong. To take its place, China will create a "provisional legislature" in Hong Kong in July 1997. This again violates the Basic Law. The Basic Law does not include any statement about a provisional legislative body. As a matter of fact, it assumes that all members of the existing Legco will serve a full term of four years until 1999.

There is yet another example that indicates China's disrespect for the law. According to the Sino-British agreement regarding the future of Hong Kong signed in December 1984, China will form a Preparatory Committee in 1996 to oversee the transfer of sovereignty. Prior to that, however, all transitional matters will be addressed by the Joint Liaison Group (JLG) composed of representatives from Britain and China; but in 1993, the mainland unilaterally established the Preliminary Working Committee (PWC) to deliberate on post-1997 affairs. This was extremely confusing to Hong Kong's citizens as well as to the local government, for the PWC, which was disbanded at the end of 1995 in anticipation of the creation of the Preparatory Committee, acted as an alternate authority to the government in Hong Kong. Yet Britain did not challenge China when it broke the law. As a matter of fact, many times Britain has also been a participant.

The Judiciary

The independence of the judiciary is highly treasured in Hong Kong; but since China is eager to intervene in Hong Kong's affairs, even before 1997, its future is questionable. In 1994, for example, the wife of an American who drowned in a hotel swimming pool in Hong Kong wanted to sue the hotel for negligence. Moreover, she successfully applied before a judge in Boston to have the case heard in the United States. The reason he gave was that the future of the legal system in Hong Kong in the years ahead is uncertain!

The quality of the judiciary has also been called into question. Until the appointment of a judiciary administrator in 1994, the administration of the judiciary was chaotic and outdated. Even today some judges have to take handwritten notes in all court proceedings. It is also true that judges have formed small circles according to race and nationality. There are at least three groups of judges: one from the United Kingdom, one from Australia and New Zealand and one local group. Favoritism has abounded in terms of promotion and duty assignments. What Anthony Duckett, an Australian judge, observed about the behavior of senior judges is not without foundation (he particularly named Sir Ti Liang Yang, Hong Kong's chief justice). According to Duckett, a former deputy director of public prosecutions in Hong Kong, ". . . His Lordship will sit through days of learned submissions from counsel without comment or response. . . . His judgments can bear little or no relationship to issues that counsel on both sides actually understood to be the subject matter of the proceedings. . . ."

Duckett was not the only person who questioned the caliber and integrity of Hong Kong's judges. Many members of the bar have openly expressed the same opinion in similar terms. That was why the bar was so insistent that China should not set a limit on the number of overseas judges who will sit on the CFA. Many judges in Hong Kong tend to give favorable judgments to lawyers on the grounds of their seniority rather than the reasoning and arguments that they put forth.

THE LEGAL PROFESSION

Lawyers and business people in Hong Kong are alike: they are both profit-oriented. The large law firms are much more interested in doing conveyancing than promoting justice. Reportedly, 70 percent to 80 percent of the lawyers are now serving firms which have business interests on the mainland. That was why the Law Society changed its stance on the CFA, from opposition to China's position in 1991 to support for it in 1995. As the president of the Law Society poignantly pointed out, the times have changed. As 1997 draws nearer, business people with interests in China, or even in Hong Kong, need to consider China's views more carefully.

Martin Lee Chu-ming, himself a queen's counsel or senior barrister, wanted to sue a retired Supreme Court judge, Simon Li Fook-sean, for libel in 1993. Li had commented that Lee should not be allowed to serve in Legco after 1997 because of his pro-democracy stance. Lee tried to find a law firm to represent him. To his annoyance, however, the four largest law firms in Hong Kong all declined. Two explained that there might be a conflict of interest; one gave no reason; and the fourth stated plainly that politically it was too sensitive to accept. There was no trace of pressure though from China; but because of commercial interests, these law firms had adopted self-censorship. When Lee complained, the Law Society said that there was no problem in the legal profession but rather that Lee was the problem!

A local newspaper editorial in June 1995 accused Hong Kong's lawyers of being greedy, not so much for charging their clients exorbitant fees, but because of their protectionist attitude. The Law Society, for instance, objected to almost every proposal outlined in the "Consultation Paper on Legal Services" in 1995 that aimed to reform the legal system in Hong Kong. According to one government source, many of the proposals were extremely mild. For example, it did not suggest that solicitors' monopoly on conveyancing should be dismantled as Britain had done several years ago, but rather it only recommended that the much criticized fixed-rate charges that are pegged to the value of the property should be eliminated.

Because of the high fees which lawyers charge in Hong Kong, justice can easily become a concept only for the rich. Several years ago a wealthy businessman, who is also a steward of the Jockey Club, was charged with fraud, and a team of lawyers defended him. He was eventually acquitted on the grounds that he was suffering from cancer and would not live for more than six months. Five years later though he is still very much alive and playing golf daily in the United States! A similar case involved the president of a Chinese bank in Hong Kong. His lawyers argued that their client was suffering from senile dementia and, therefore, the court proceedings should be discontinued. The court accepted, and this gentleman was seen conducting the 1995 annual meeting of the bank by television viewers. It is not unusual for a senior barrister to charge HK$250,000 to HK$500,000 (US$32,051 to US$64,102) for a simple case. Consequently, it is not surprising that both former attorney generals in Hong Kong have decided to enter private practice.

Law Enforcement

The rule of law says that no one is above the law. However, governments throughout the world seem to think that only its citizens need to abide by the law. A magistrate in 1995, for example, ruled that Section 30 of the ICAC Ordinance, which forbids the media to disclose the names of those being investigated, contravened the Bill of Rights; and on this ground, he acquitted *Ming Pao's* publisher. Immediately after the verdict, the ICAC issued a statement saying that since, unlike the rulings of the Supreme Court, the magistrate's ruling is not binding the ICAC will continue to use Section 30.

Because the Hong Kong government is not accountable to the general public, oftentimes it overlooks the importance of maintaining checks and balances within its system. A case in point is the Complaints against Police Office (CAPO), which is presently a unit in the police department. It has little credibility as it is perceived by the general public that the police cannot investigate the wrongdoings of their colleagues. Thus, Legco voted in 1994 to ask the government to make CAPO independent of the police. Their argument was extremely simple: if the police investigate the police, who investigates the police force? The government, however, decided to ignore Legco's plea.

The Legal Department has not been immune from these types of problems either. Until the end of 1994, the department was controlled and staffed by expatriates. In recent years, it has been plagued by numerous scandals. A director who was responsible for determining whether a case should proceed for prosecution was convicted and sent to prison for eight years for accepting bribes. Unless the government decides to revamp the Legal Department, the "rule of law" may soon become an empty slogan.

Because of a relatively uncertain future, a great many senior law enforcement officers have resigned in recent years. This has brought undesirable and negative effects on the enforcement of the law in Hong Kong. A case in point is the police. Over a period of several months in 1995, there were two fatal shooting incidents involving two new officers on the police force. An unarmed youth suspected of burglary and a 60-year old handicapped man were shot dead. The year before a physically handicapped businessman from south Korea was also killed by a police officer while being held hostage in a taxi. Inexperienced officers greatly impair the administration of justice in the territory.

Corruption and Organized Crime

Just in the month of September 1995, the ICAC successfully brought officers from three different disciplined forces to trial. One case involved 10 health inspectors who issued or withheld restaurant licenses and passed or failed the regular hygiene inspections at eating establishments based upon whether or not they were bribed. The ICAC commented that the whole operation was well-organized and even syndicated. In another case, about five police officers were arrested in an extortion racket managed by triad elements in decorating companies in public housing estates. Lastly, a chief police inspector, a sergeant and two other officers were apprehended for receiving HK$500,000 (US$64,103) from brothel operators as protection money.

In addition to these cases, the community had just learned at the time that 70 police officers were involved in a male prostitution racket. This not only greatly damaged the image of the Hong Kong police but also raised the question of how frequently officers were engaged in off-duty activities. Furthermore, three other serving officers were charged with robbery.

Toward the end of 1995, the ICAC issued a warning that because of 1997 many law enforcement officers wanted to make extra money and, as a result, got themselves intwined in corrupt practices. For the first eight months of 1995, the ICAC reported that its caseload was more than 160 percent higher than 1994! According to the police force, by the end of September of that year, 60 police officers were being investigated internally, and 136 had been suspended awaiting further investigation and action. The chief of police also admitted that police officers who are in debt (primarily because of heavy gambling) have become a very serious problem as well. One major contributing factor is due to the loose supervisory system within the disciplined forces; the other cause regards the low morale of senior officers.

The private sector is also plagued by corruption. According to one survey in 1995, 80 percent of the employees questioned believed that their firms were corrupt. This was an increase of 10 percent compared with the same survey taken in the previous year. Moreover, the ICAC revealed that for the first eight months of 1995 there were 225 cases involving corruption in the private sector that were brought to court. During the whole year of 1994, there were only 160 such prosecutions!

The Hong Kong government has insisted that Hong Kong is still a very safe city. The crime rate is relatively low compared with other large cities in the world. The rule of law is very much intact despite the ICAC's recent warning, but the upsurge of corruption among the disciplined forces is very worrisome. If not checked, the rule of law in Hong Kong will become a recollection of the past.

The increased activities of the underworld should be another concern in Hong Kong. Principals often complain that triad elements have infiltrated many of their schools. It is also no secret that organized crime is heavily involved in the entertainment industry. Is organized crime in Hong Kong blessed by China though?

It is a fact that whatever China's leaders have said and done in recent years has had serious implications in Hong Kong. In 1993, Tao Siju, China's head of public security, admitted to Hong Kong reporters that the security bureau had regular contacts with the triads in Hong Kong. He reiterated the thoughts of Deng Xiaoping in October 1984 when he said that there are also good and patriotic elements in the underworld.

Deng's statement was made in the Great Hall of the People in front of 200 prominent Hong Kong citizens. He tried to answer a question raised by the audience: "Who among Hong Kong's citizens could rule Hong Kong?"

"As long as they are patriotic," Deng replied, "any Hong Kong citizen - business tycoons, professionals or even triad members - could rule Hong Kong after 1997. There are also patriotic elements in the triad societies." (Reportedly, Deng had a good experience with the triads during his visit to the United States in 1979. The Chinese triads there had mobilized 800 members to protect Deng throughout his trip!)

This, therefore, raises another element of anxiety in the community. If corrupt officials and organized crime remain unchecked in the near future, Hong Kong's rule of law will be further undermined.

The Problem of Localization

Finally, the rule of law has to depend on the awareness of the general public that each and every person has to respect and abide by the law. The approach which the Hong Kong government has taken in the past has concentrated too much on the enforcement of the law, i.e., to punish the people who break the law. A far superior approach is to enhance the understanding of the legal system in the minds of ordinary citizens. The government has done far too little in this area. Law Week, organized by the legal profession, can hardly reach the community's grassroots people.

One of the prerequisites to popularize legal knowledge is to localize the whole legal system in Hong Kong, to make the system less British and more Hong Kong Chinese. This should include reforming the laws which are inconsistent with the Hong Kong context, translating the laws into Chinese, conducting court proceedings in Cantonese, especially in the courts which deal with criminal cases, and, above all, accelerating the process of appointing more local lawyers to be judges or prosecutors. The last measure is especially difficult because local lawyers favor private practice over public service. It is also a matter of supply and demand. In order to attract more qualified people to public service, the Hong Kong government should seriously consider giving its judges and lawyers more lucrative terms of service. The community should be prepared to put more resources into the whole localization process.

The rule of law says that justice must not only be rightly administered but also must be seen to be done by the public. It is an important requirement of any legal system that the rule of law must protect the innocent. One of the characteristics of common law is that all people are presumed innocent until proven guilty. This is in line with international human rights provisions. In Hong Kong, legal aid is given to those who cannot afford to engage private legal representation. However, the Legal Aid Department will better serve the public if it is made independent. Once divorced from the government, the Legal Aid Department will not only be more trusted by the public but will also be in a better position to do much more in terms of legal reform advocacy and the advocacy of the rule of law.

DIFFERENT VALUES, DIFFERENT DEFINITIONS

FREEDOMS NOT LEGALLY GUARANTEED

Hong Kong has a relatively benevolent government which is answerable to the British government, one of the oldest democracies in the world. For more than 150 years, the residents of Hong Kong have enjoyed a relatively broad spectrum of freedoms, at least by Asian standards. As long as they did not challenge the government or law enforcement authorities, they could do whatever they liked. However, these freedoms and rights are not fully entrenched in the territory's legal system; and as a colonial government, it still maintains many draconian laws, though when challenged the government replies that these are only used sparingly. However, as 1997 draws nearer and as China increases its pressure on the territory, the Hong Kong government has invoked them regularly over the past six years.

In February 1990, for instance, six democratic leaders in Hong Kong staged a sit-in at the Star Ferry on the Kowloon side of the harbor and protested against the promulgation of an "undemocratic Basic Law" that was being considered by China's National People's Congress (NPC). The Hong Kong government decided to prosecute the demonstrators, charging them with using loudspeakers in a public place without a permit issued by the police commissioner and with collecting donations in a public place without a permit issued by the director of the Social Welfare Department. The wider community in Hong Kong was bewildered as to why the government would take such relatively trivial legal actions against these six highly respected democratic leaders, five of whom are now elected members of the Legislative Council (Legco). The answer is simple: China had exerted tremendous pressure on the Hong Kong government and had asked them to suppress all dissenting voices against the Basic Law. Even today the Public Order Ordinance remains a draconian law which the Hong Kong government invokes when it considers necessary.

Moreover, in the summer of 1991, the Hong Kong Federation of Students (HKFS) decided to host the second conference of overseas Chinese students after the violent suppression of dissent in Tiananmen Square. Again, because of pressure from China, the Hong Kong government decided to sabotage the conference by withholding its permission for 15 Chinese students to enter Hong Kong despite the fact that they all held valid visas. The law which it invoked was the Immigration Ordinance, which gives the director of immigration the right to deny entry to anyone without a corresponding need to state the reasons for his decision.

Furthermore, a Taiwanese film the same year depicting the Cultural Revolution on the mainland in the 1960s was banned from being shown publicly in Hong Kong. The Film Censorship Ordinance which the government invoked stated that the authorities reserve the right to ban any film which may harm any neighboring country, meaning, of course, China.

Previously the Urban Council had rejected in a similar fashion a request from a Christian group in 1990 to hold a prayer meeting to commemorate those who died during the crackdown on June 4, 1989, in Tiananmen Square. The group wanted to hold the prayer meeting in a stadium across the street from the New China News Agency (NCNA), China's *de facto* consulate in Hong Kong. The Urban Council used no law to justify itself, for it is the usual practice of the administrator to make rulings without divulging any reason for the decision, like the directors of many government departments.

In addition, law enforcement officers in Hong Kong are given extensive powers, which means civil liberties are often curtailed. Officers from the Independent Commission against Corruption (ICAC), for example, mercilessly intrude upon the privacy of the people that they investigate. It is also not uncommon to see police constables stop passersby on the streets to check their identity cards. If the officers suspect that the person they confront is an illegal immigrant or criminal, a body search is also conducted. Oftentimes this is quite embarrassing and humiliating. In a well-publicized case in 1995, English and Irish Derby-winning jockey Alan Munro spent a whole afternoon staring at the walls of a Tsim Sha Tsui police cell because he failed to prove his identity.

There are many other draconian laws among Hong Kong's statutes as well. Even if we accept the fact that the present Hong Kong government, which is answerable to the British government, very rarely uses these laws, conditions may change after 1997, for the value system of the Chinese government is quite different from that of the British. The Chinese leaders often claim that in China the right to survival is far more important than civil liberties. By this, they mean that they should be given more power and the people less. For outsiders, it is difficult to follow this kind of logic. As a whole, people are more productive if they are given more freedom and responsibilities. After 1997, the Chinese authorities can easily use the Official Secrets Act or the State Emergency Act, which are colonial and archaic, to put dissidents in jail without a proper trial. The British government, in fact, has since amended them in the United Kingdom.

Furthermore, after 1997, the Hong Kong Special Administrative Region (SAR) has no jurisdiction over so-called "acts of state." The Chinese authorities can define an act of state in such a way so as to silence any dissent and criticism. In addition, the interpretation of the Basic Law, the mini-Constitution for post-1997 Hong Kong, does not rest with Hong Kong's Court of Final Appeal (CFA); the Standing Committee of the NPC has that power. This greatly hinders Hong Kong's judicial independence. These should be very important issues for the citizens of Hong Kong as well as for all of those who do business in Hong Kong or who wish to invest in the territory.

In another area of concern, the British government, in answering a question by the United Nations Human Rights Commission in 1991, promised to do much more in the area of human rights education. To put this promise into practice, it should begin with Hong Kong's law enforcement officers, for overall, the law enforcement personnel in the territory have a very vague idea about human rights nor are they eager to promote human rights in Hong Kong because, according to them, the more that citizens are aware of their rights, the more difficult their job becomes.

THE BILL OF RIGHTS

After several years of campaigning by concerned groups and pressure from the British government, the Hong Kong legislature finally enacted the Bill of Rights in June 1991. It did not generate much excitement in Hong Kong though for no one expected the bill to bring any major change to the territory. Law enforcement personnel as well as the business community, however, expressed their concern that the bill would have negative effects on law and order in the territory, and China strongly berated Britain for introducing it.

As for the provisions of the legislation, it is far below international standards. Basically, the Bill of Rights only includes the conditions contained in the International Covenant on Civil and Political Rights (ICCPR): it does not incorporate any provisions of the International Covenant on Economic, Social and Cultural

Rights (ICESCR). The explanation given by the Hong Kong government: "ICESCR rights are not rights that can be easily enforced by the courts."

The fact that the provisions of the ICESCR are not included in the Bill of Rights does not exonerate the Hong Kong government from recognizing the economic, social and cultural rights of its citizens, however. In 1976, Britain ratified the ICESCR and extended these rights to Hong Kong. In the November 1994 meeting of the United Nations Commission on Economic, Social and Cultural Rights, Hong Kong's implementation of these rights was seriously scrutinized. The commission's report was critical of the Hong Kong government. The overall tone of the report was that Hong Kong is a very affluent society, yet the rights of the poor, the elderly and those of racial minority groups are not adequately addressed and protected. For instance, several thousand single people still live in "caged homes" - enclosed three-tiered bunk beds that are rented to three individuals - and elderly people who depend on Comprehensive Social Security Assistance (CSSA) have only a shameful HK$60 (US$7.69) per day to meet their daily needs.

When the government introduced the Bill of Rights, it claimed that it copied word for word the provisions found in the ICCPR. However, it seems that there are at least two very important omissions. One is the right of "self-determination" found in Article 1, Clause 1 of the ICCPR. Hong Kong citizens are deprived of this right totally. Even when China and Britain were negotiating the future of Hong Kong, the people were not consulted. In lamenting this fact, a senior political leader in Hong Kong, Baroness Lydia Dunn, pointed out a decade ago that Britain has only the right to return the land but not its citizens to China.

The other omission concerns the political rights of the people. Article 25 of the ICCPR states that every citizen has the "right to take part in the conduct of public affairs, directly or through freely chosen representatives," and "to vote and to be elected at genuine periodic elections which shall be by universal and equal suffrage. . . ." The fact is that currently the governor is appointed and more than two-thirds of the legislative councillors are not directly elected by the people, violating the stipulations of the ICCPR. The post-1997 SAR will basically follow the same model, except that the chief executive will be appointed by Beijing instead of London.

Hong Kong is on the doorstep of the fifth anniversary of the Bill of Rights' introduction in Legco. Little progress has been made in terms of advocacy, amendments to existing laws which contravene the legislation as well as mass education. In addition, the government continues to ignore popular demands for the immediate establishment of a Human Rights Commission. With no mechanism in place to enforce the Bill of Rights, Hong Kong now has only an impotent piece of legislation.

From the outset, in order to dilute the impact of the Bill of Rights, the Hong Kong government decided not to give it supremacy status, i.e., it is not above other laws in Hong Kong, nor is it firmly entrenched in the legal system; for by the vote of a simple majority in the legislature, it can be amended or even repealed. Repeatedly, China has threatened to take this latter step after 1997. If China's threat becomes reality, an important bulwark in the safeguarding of human rights in Hong Kong will be erased.

Furthermore, on more than one occasion, senior Chinese officials have stated that China has no obligation to report to the United Nations Human Rights Commission about the implementation of the two international covenants on human rights in Hong Kong - the ICCPR and the ICESCR. These threats further damage the confidence of Hong Kong's citizens. For without having to report to the commission, China can close its doors and do whatever it wants in Hong Kong. Of course, threats of this kind are inconsistent with both the Joint Declaration and Basic Law. According to Article 39 of the Basic Law, for example, "the two international covenants, as applied to Hong Kong, shall remain in force and shall be implemented through the laws of the Hong Kong Special Administrative Region." Moreover, according to Article 40 of the ICCPR and Article 18 of the ICESCR, the sovereign government of Hong Kong is duty-bound to make regular reports to the United Nations Human Rights Commission.

We must also take note of the shameful reality that Britain has abdicated its legal as well as moral responsibility in depriving 3.3 million Hong Kong Chinese citizens who were born in its territory their U.K. citizenship rights. China, meanwhile, says these people are not Chinese nationals, at least not until after 1997. Britain claims these people are British Nationals Overseas (BNO), but BNO is only the name of a passport rather than the name of a nationality. Seemingly, Britain's actions have all but rendered these 3.3 million people "stateless." This contravenes Article 24 of the ICCPR which states that "every child has the right to acquire a nationality."

Article XIX

To a great many concerned people throughout the world, Article 19 of the ICCPR pertains to the most fundamental right of human beings, namely, the right to express themselves. In fact, there is a reputable international organization called Article XIX based in London. The main aim of Article XIX is to find ways to promote this basic right for people all over the world. It often works with local groups to expose laws, incidents, etc., which adversely affect the right to freedom of expression.

Article 19 of the ICCPR states:

"(1) Everyone shall have the right to hold opinions without interference.

"(2) Everyone shall have the right to freedom of expression. This right shall include the freedom to seek, receive and impart information and ideas of all kinds, regardless of frontiers, either orally, in writing or in print, in the form of art or through any other media of his [or her] choice.

"(3) The exercise of the rights provided for in (2) carries with it special duties and responsibilities. It may, therefore, be subject to certain restrictions, but these shall only be such as are provided for by law and are necessary: (a) for respect of the rights or reputation of others and (b) for the protection of national security or of public order or of public health or morals."

Freedom of expression is very important as a basic human right; for without it, all other human rights are not possible. That explains why in a totalitarian government the first thing it withholds from the people is their right of free expression. It is through exercising their freedom of expression that people can generate a wealth of ideas. Many of these ideas will be different from those of the totalitarian rulers, which, to them, is very dangerous, for it not only makes their rule more difficult but also threatens their authority and position. Thus, in China, we have seen how Mao Zedong removed Liu Shaoji and Lin Biao and the way in which Zhao Ziyang and Hu Yaobang were purged in the 1980s. Totalitarian rulers can only tolerate people who speak their language; but without diverse views, or even criticism, it is difficult to achieve progress. New ideas can only come about when people are encouraged to think independently without any inhibition. Christine Loh Kung-wai, a highly popular legislative councillor, has often been quoted as saying, "If you are in private business and your boss tells you the company does not want more ideas and opinions from its employees and customers because they would hinder the firm's progress, you might well conclude it is time to move on."

Generally, however, people in Hong Kong can freely express themselves. Thousands of books and hundreds of magazines and journals are published weekly or monthly. There are at least a dozen reputable daily newspapers (nine in Chinese and three in English). Citizens can and do write letters to the editors of newspapers and journals and do participate actively in several daily radio phone-in programs. Despite having all of these means to express their views, there is still a need for improvement. In a way, because of the hesitancy of the Hong Kong government, Hong Kong has lost several golden opportunities to become a more open society.

First, despite the fact that Hong Kong is highly regarded as a global telecommunications hub as well as a champion of freedom of expression, it does not yet have a public access television channel. In the early 1990s when the government franchised cable television to the Wharf consortium, Wharf was obliged to provide three channels for government or public use. The government, with very low administrative costs, could have assigned one as a public access channel. This could have encouraged the public to air their ideas and opinions through the production of their own television programs, for now television air time is terribly expensive and is monopolized by Big Business. However, in anticipation of China's strong objection to such a move and to keep the liberal critics of government at bay, the authorities finally decided to go against the wishes of the public and Legco, which had voted in favor of providing such a public channel.

Second, at about the same time that it awarded the cable television franchise, the government wanted to privatize Radio Television Hong Kong (RTHK) to produce a local media organization similar to the BBC in Britain. This was in line with the government's aim to trim its involvement and increase public participation. As expected, however, the Chinese government raised strong objections; for to China, the media is to serve the government, especially the party, rather than the public. The government, therefore, must be in full control of its own mouthpiece. To allow RTHK to become independent certainly was against the interests of China which, at that time, would be assuming sovereignty over Hong Kong in just a few years. Since the Hong Kong government did not want to create another confrontation with the mainland, this proposal was abandoned.

Third, in 1993, Christine Loh put a lot of effort into trying to introduce the Access of Information Bill as a private member's bill in Legco. Her intent was to make the government more open and to ensure that the right of citizens to information was protected by law. The government, however, chose not to accede to such a bill but instead promised to achieve the same result through issuing executive orders that made information in certain departments, such as Social Welfare, Public Works, etc., available to the public. The shortcoming of this approach is that decisions over which departments will become more transparent and what information will be released to the public are left to the government. Loh's bill would have held all government departments to the same standard of disclosure.

FREEDOM OF THE PRESS

In order to generate freedom of expression, a free press is of the utmost importance. A free press can help ensure that the government does its job properly, serving the interests of all citizens rather than simply a small segment of the people, such as the business community. A free press can also help engender the public's interest in engaging in active and informed discussion about Hong Kong's future.

Today, although the press in Hong Kong in general is free, the atmosphere is beginning to change.

First of all, the morale of the local press corps is falling. The wages of reporters working for most of the Chinese newspapers are very meager, but the workload is heavy. Increasingly, those who cover local government affairs as well as events in China have become extremely disillusioned. According to a survey conducted by the School of Journalism at the Chinese University of Hong Kong in 1990, 50 percent of the reporters said that they were very careful when writing any stories related to China, and 25 percent said that they would not write anything which might offend China.

Moreover, the turnover rate of reporters is exceptionally high. This adversely affects the quality of the media. According to a survey conducted by the Social Services Research Center at Hong Kong University in 1995, only 42 percent of Hong Kong's citizens believe the news media behaves responsibly, sharply down from 59 percent in a similar survey the previous year, and only 53 percent believe the press acts professionally, down from 62 percent in 1994.

Another factor which may have an adverse effect on freedom of the press in Hong Kong is the fact that more and more business tycoons have taken control of several major newspapers. In other words, the media is no longer controlled by journalists or by those who are professionally aware of what is vital to a vibrant press. Robert Kuok, a Malaysian businessman, for instance, won control of the *South China Morning Post* in 1992; three years later another Malaysian business tycoon, Tiong Hien-king, became the new owner of *Ming Pao*. These are two of the most influential newspapers in the territory - the first published in English, the second in Chinese. Since both Kuok and Tiong have extensive commercial interests in mainland China, many fear that eventually their publications' independent editorial policy will give way to a pro-China stance.

Self-censorship - now not uncommon in Hong Kong - is also a concern. Since most of the important print and electronic media in Hong Kong are controlled by pro-China business people, it is unrealistic to expect Hong Kong to continue to enjoy an independent, impartial and outspoken media. Asian Television's (ATV) *News Tease*, an extremely popular talk show that was highly critical of China, was canceled. ATV also decided not to broadcast a Spanish documentary on the Beijing massacre in

1989, and Television Broadcasts (TVB) voluntarily withdrew the viewing of a BBC documentary about Mao Zedong. In fact, both documentaries were not at all critical of China, and yet, for fear of arousing China's displeasure, the management of both ATV and TVB overruled the decisions of their staff.

To China, the media is the mouthpiece of the authorities, whether television, radio, newspapers or magazines. Even when officials are not directly managing them, the authorities must reserve the right of "censorship." Consequently, the media cannot be independent. Members of the press corps in Hong Kong who have worked on the mainland have been exposed to this system for the past several years. After June 1989, China announced "seven principles" for Hong Kong reporters who want to cover a story on the mainland. Consistently, China has refused permission for "unfriendly" journalists from Hong Kong to report about events on the mainland, and many Hong Kong reporters have had experiences of being harassed. In a prominent case in 1994, a Hong Kong reporter, Xi Yang, was jailed for 12 years after being convicted of stealing state financial secrets. Many viewed this as a stern warning to Hong Kong's reporters to behave. To China's leaders, the more the journalists are intimidated, the less the public in Hong Kong will know!

Press freedom in Hong Kong is, thus, deteriorating rapidly because of intimidation from China and self-censorship adopted by local journalists. This is not in Hong Kong's public interest. The freedom of expression that citizens now enjoy will be greatly curtailed if Hong Kong's press freedom is restricted or denied.

UNEQUAL RIGHTS

Despite its status as a modern and international city, discrimination in Hong Kong based on sex, age, race, class, etc., abounds. In order to outlaw all forms of discrimination, Legislative Councillor Anna Wu Hung-yuk worked tirelessly for a year to try to introduce the Equal Opportunities Bill and the Human Rights and Equal Opportunities Commission Bill in Legco.

At the outset, the governor blocked Wu's effort to introduce the second bill that sought to establish a Human Rights Commission on the grounds that it had financial implications as Legco members can only introduce a private member's bill if it does not require the government to increase its budget. Then, in order to dissuade Wu from introducing the Equal Opportunities Bill, the government hurriedly introduced two bills which aimed to outlaw discrimination based on sex and disability. Unperturbed, Wu persisted and drafted three other bills that sought to eliminate discrimination based on "age, race, religious or political convictions, union activities and spent criminal convictions." After a year's consultation and study, they finally went to the last session of the 1994-1995 sitting of Legco in July 1995. Without extensive debate, the government coerced the business-biased legislature to vote down all three bills submitted by Wu. The pro-business legislators argued that there were liberal values implicit in the provisions of Wu's bills. If enacted, there would be many unnecessary disputes and legal proceedings. In turn, Hong Kong's social harmony would be upset. Thus, to them, the best way to proceed was not by legislation but through education.

The main arguments offered by the government, however, were even more absurd. It argued that, though it was in favor of promoting equal opportunities for every citizen, Wu's bills belonged to a new area of law in Hong Kong; therefore, it needed more time to study them.

Consequently, Hong Kong is far from being a city where there are equal opportunities for all. The Convention on the Elimination of All Forms of Discrimination against Women (CEDAW) is yet to be extended to Hong Kong despite the fact that both Britain and China are signatories, and many racial minority groups are treated badly by some local Chinese people. For example, the 148,000 women who work in Hong Kong as domestic helpers - 83 percent of whom are from the Philippines - are subject to the government's two-week rule that deters them from leaving their jobs even if they are mistreated by their employers. Furthermore, as a result of pressure from the employers of domestic workers, the government refused to adjust, as in previous years, their minimum wage of HK$3,750 (US$481) per month. Yet Hong Kong's inflation rate for the year 1995 was 8.5 percent!

As for other overseas laborers, it is not uncommon to learn that they are being underpaid or cheated in some other manner. The *South China Morning Post* revealed at the end of September 1995 that almost all of the Thai construction workers hired for the new airport-related projects received wage deductions of up to 50 percent; yet according to their contracts, their employers cannot deduct more than 25 percent of their wages for room and board.

Hong Kong cannot be considered a truly fair society until exploitation ends, until all of its citizens enjoy equal opportunities. Only when the basic rights of everyone, including the weak, the handicapped and minorities, are respected and protected can Hong Kong claim that it is a caring community.

IN SEARCH OF REPRESENTATIVE GOVERNMENT

TOO LITTLE, TOO LATE

It has often been said that despite an absence of democracy there are plenty of freedoms for the citizens of Hong Kong; for although the territory is a British Crown Colony and its government is colonial - hence, not answerable to the people of Hong Kong - it is accountable to the British government, which is the world's oldest democracy.

It is not entirely true to say that the British government has never had any intention of instituting democracy in Hong Kong. Mark Young, a former governor of Hong Kong (1941-1947), tried, for example, to introduce some form of democracy in the Legislative Council (Legco) elections after the Second World War; but because of the turbulence and civil war in mainland China at the time, the British government decided to postpone its plans for more democratic participation in the territory.

The Chinese-instigated riots in 1967, however, forced the Hong Kong government to open up its rather obsolete form of government. As a result, government by consultation was introduced. In order to solicit opinions from grassroots citizens, district offices were established. A rather comprehensive advisory system was also instituted, and at least one advisory committee was formed in every government department. Dennis Bray, a former home affairs secretary, used to say that there were 12 channels for the government to solicit views from its citizens.

When Britain realized, however, that it was unrealistic to prolong its rule in Hong Kong beyond 1997, it made preparations in at least two broad areas. One was to ensure that Hong Kong's citizens would not flood the British Isles, even during the worst-case scenario; the other was to try to build a political system in Hong Kong whereby it would still be "British" although the territory's colonial administration no longer existed. The British government was fully aware, of course, that unless Hong Kong's people were given more political power the system which they had built over a period of more than 150 years would be ruined overnight in 1997.

The first step the British took was to introduce district administration in Hong Kong. A White Paper was published in January 1981, and the first district board elections took place in Kwun Tong in 1982. Since then, district boards have been established in every district with 18 presently in existence. The functions of district boards are very limited, however - the primary purpose being to advise the central government regarding district affairs.

The second step was to introduce "representative government" in Hong Kong. The White Paper entitled "The Further Development of Representative Government in Hong Kong" was published in November 1984. Its major objectives were "(a) to develop progressively a system of government, the authority for which is firmly rooted in Hong Kong, which is able to represent authoritatively the views of the people of Hong Kong and which is more directly accountable to the people of Hong Kong, (b) to build this system on our existing institutions, which have served Hong Kong well, and, as far as possible, to preserve their best features, including the maintenance of the well-established practice of government by consensus, and (c) to allow for further development if that should be the wish of the community." The paper further stated that the government should adopt "a cautious approach with a gradual start by introducing a very small number of directly elected members in Legco in 1988 and building up to a significant number of directly elected members by 1997." Because of China's vehement objections, however, the paper's proposals were quashed.

In the meantime, the Hong Kong government concentrated on building a relationship of mutual understanding and cooperation with Legco over policies and programs. This was its idea of government by consensus. It was easy to do because as late as 1991 most Legco members were appointed by the governor. However, this consensus was based only on agreement between senior government officials and the business community that the appointed Legco members represented: Legco did not truly represent the wider community of Hong Kong.

Thus, in this context of diluted democracy, the first elections to Legco took place in 1985. Twelve legislative councilors were elected from the functional constituencies representing primarily the business community and professional groups, and 12 were chosen from the district boards and two municipal councils. The remaining 32 Legco members were either appointed by the governor or were government officials themselves.

Direct elections, as understood by most of the world where some form of democracy is entrenched, were only introduced in 1991. In this election, 18 members in the 60-member legislative body were elected from nine geographical constituencies. This first electoral exercise by the people was followed four years later with another Legco election in September 1995 - the last election before the transfer of sovereignty in 1997 and the only election to be based on Gov. Chris Patten's political reform package - in which this number was marginally increased to 20 seats. The remaining Legco members in this election were determined as follows: 30 from the functional constituencies and 10 by the Election Committee comprised of 283 district board members.

Undoubtedly, the British government made an extremely late start in introducing any form of democracy in Hong Kong. Even then, the steps it has taken have been extremely small. The British government has had no intention of opening the executive-led government in the territory to the general public. All it wanted was to build a checks-and-balances mechanism, to have an elected Legco to monitor closely the government's performance.

China, however, has stated that it will not accept this arrangement instituted by the British: it will dismantle Legco in July 1997. If China proceeds with this threat, it will be a genuine setback for the democratic development of Hong Kong. More than 920,000 citizens cared enough to take part in the poll in September 1995. In an extremely orderly way, they elected their representatives to Legco. China cannot deprive Hong Kong's citizens of their most basic political rights.

However, being Hong Kong's current sovereign government, Britain did not forcefully confront China's challenge. Qian Qichen, the Chinese vice premier and foreign minister, was in London in early October 1995 to meet with his British counterpart Malcolm Rifkin. Reportedly, Rifkin did not question Qian on the issue of Hong Kong's legislative "through train" that would permit those elected in 1995 to serve their full four-year terms under both the present and future government. Perhaps Rifkin was too busy discussing Sino-British trade deals. Martin Lee Chu-ming, a leading democrat in Hong Kong, is justified in accusing the British of trying to destroy the Legco they have tried to build in the last decade.

GROWING ASPIRATIONS

Of the 6.3 million citizens in Hong Kong, more than 90 percent are ethic Chinese. They have Chinese blood, and their mindset is greatly influenced by Chinese culture and its traditions. Historically, China has been an agrarian society; most of the people have lived in the countryside and have conducted a simple life. A Chinese poem describes their lifestyle and outlook on their world:

"When the sun rises,
They go to the fields and work.
When the sun sets,
They go home to rest.
In order to have food,
They work in the fields.
In order to have water to drink,
They drill wells.
The emperor is too far away
To have anything to do with them."

Thus, by and large, Chinese people have not been interested in public affairs nor in those who administer them. There is another Chinese saying: "When you are alive, avoid going to a government office. When you are dead, avoid going to hell." Government officials represent "authority"; the Chinese people are extremely nervous about those who hold this authority. Moreover, Chinese people are only concerned about their own family or clan. Another Chinese proverb says, "Every family is responsible for sweeping the snow in front of its house. Never mind about the sleet fallen on the neighbor's home."

Because of this feeling of alienation between the government and the governed, over the long centuries, the governed literally have surrendered their rights to government officials. Traditionally, emperors viewed their citizens as "ants" (of little value) and demanded absolute loyalty from their subjects. Another Chinese expression describes this very vividly: "When the emperor demands that you die, if you refuse to die, you are disloyal to your emperor."

Thus, being "Chinese," Hong Kong's citizens are apathetic to public affairs. For those who were born and educated in Hong Kong, however, they are at an even greater disadvantage, for the colonial education system has taught them to be obedient and to never challenge government authorities. Consequently, Hong Kong's students are very good at memorizing facts but poor in independent thinking. Children in Hong Kong are only taught to work hard and when they finish school to try their best to climb high on the social ladder.

Moreover, as a colony, Hong Kong is a "borrowed place"; few citizens have a strong sense of belonging. Chinese people come to the territory to make money. They are happy to leave "everything else" to the government.

Unfortunately, the Church in Hong Kong has not offered any new direction or guidance in this regard. With 50 percent of the children educated in high schools operated by the Church, it is in a position of great influence in the community. Being a conservative institution, however, it has chosen to only teach its students to follow the rules and never to raise questions or cause trouble. Thus, it acts to reinforce the status quo.

However, the times have changed in recent years; Hong Kong has become more affluent. Many young local professionals and entrepreneurs who were trained in the West are not satisfied with only material rewards. They want to participate in determining Hong Kong's future, which is theirs as well, for they consider Hong Kong their home, not just a place to sojourn. They are ready to assume more responsibility. Some have even thrown themselves into the struggle for a faster pace of democracy in Hong Kong.

WHY DEMOCRACY NOW?

Many pro-Beijing citizens in Hong Kong argue forcefully that Hong Kong has been running well for more than 150 years without a democratic political structure so why should such a system be introduced now? Their arguments are echoed in general by many business leaders who are heavily involved in trade with

China or who have investments on the mainland and who consider democracy to be an unnecessary intrusion that may revoke many of the privileges that they have enjoyed under a colonial, elitist appointment political system. Let us examine the issue more objectively, however.

First, Hong Kong has become one of the most important trading entities and one of the leading financial centers in the world. It needs the support of a more open political system. An archaic political framework which cannot represent authoritatively the views of Hong Kong's people and is not accountable to its citizens is not suitable for the city's level of sophistication. In reality, Hong Kong can no longer rely solely on the handful of business tycoons and their associates to make all vital decisions for the community. The working class must be represented as well. Only when all segments of society are given a chance to work together can Hong Kong enjoy long-term stability and prosperity; for as it continues to move forward, the territory needs the full support and contribution of citizens from all walks of life. Only an open, fair and participatory political system accepted by the majority of its citizens can entice them to work and, when necessary, to sacrifice for the good of Hong Kong.

Furthermore, if Hong Kong wants to be free from corruption, which presently abounds on the mainland, no person or group of people can be allowed to have unchecked power. Only a democratically elected government can prevent those in power from abusing it.

Second, according to all major opinion polls in recent years, the dominant concern of Hong Kong's citizens about 1997 is not the lowering of their living standards nor even the loss of their wealth but rather the diminishing of their personal freedoms.

In order to safeguard people's individual freedoms, a respect for the rule of law and an independent judiciary are both essential. By and large, both are prevalent in Hong Kong now. Moreover, the present government, influenced by and accountable to the British government, oftentimes is expected by London to rule Hong Kong with democratic values and principles. After 1997, however, the Hong Kong government will not be constrained by the same expectations nor by the same values and principles, for the historical development of China and the reservoir of values and principles that it has engendered is vastly different from those of Britain. Thus, the only solution is to build a democratic political system in Hong Kong that will reflect the wishes of its people. Only a government elected by its people and accountable to them is likely to protect the basic rights and freedoms of its citizens. That being the case, Hong Kong's citizens expect their existing government to set standards for the future Special Administrative Region (SAR) government to safeguard their basic rights and freedoms. That is why democracy is urgently needed in Hong Kong today.

While the three guiding principles - "one country, two systems," "a highly autonomous government" and "Hong Kong people ruling Hong Kong" - form the basis of the Sino-British Joint Declaration signed in December 1984, we must also uphold its call for an elected legislature in post-1997 Hong Kong and a future executive branch of government that is answerable to Legco. All of these vital points are also included in the Basic Law promulgated in April 1990. In other words, democracy is what has been promised to the people of Hong Kong by both Britain and China.

It has often been argued that Beijing wants the world to know that it is China which will bequeath democracy to Hong Kong, and consequently, the mainland opposes any attempt by the British to grant too much democracy to Hong Kong before 1997. The fact is though that replacing a colonial government with a democratic government involves many radical changes. It is better for Hong Kong if these reforms are introduced gradually. The territory cannot have a fully elected government overnight.

That is why it is necessary to introduce democracy in Hong Kong as early as possible. This view is widely shared by British politicians, including former Prime Minister Edward Heath.

Future Prospects

In its stated desire to establish a representative government in the territory, the Hong Kong government was moving in the right direction in the mid-1980s. Its policy paper "The Further Development of Representative Government in Hong Kong" published in November 1984 was hailed as a milestone in the democratic journey of Hong Kong. At its present stage of development, Hong Kong needs a fully representative government, for only with such a government can Hong Kong move forward with confidence. In order to be able to represent the people authoritatively, it must be elected directly by the people, and it must respond to the wishes and needs of the wider community and not just a small segment of the population. A fully representative government can engender wider concern and participation by the people as a whole. Although a representative government may not perfectly permit the direct participation of people in decision making, it can minimize the abuses of power of government officials and can better safeguard citizens' basic rights and freedoms. Without a representative government, the rule of law and civil liberties can easily be suppressed.

While the goal set forth by the Hong Kong government in the 1984 policy paper was laudable, officials did not go far enough in making their goal of representative government a reality. The paper itself only suggested ways to open up the legislature "by introducing a very small number of directly elected members in 1988 and building up to a significant number of directly elected members by 1997," but nothing was proposed for the executive branch; for ever since its beginnings as a British Crown Colony in 1843, Hong Kong's governors have all been appointed by London. As a representative of the British government, the Hong

Kong governor is duty-bound to protect British interests first rather than the interests of the people of Hong Kong. Former Gov. David Wilson, for instance, wanted to ignore the objections of China and proceed with the Port and Airport Development Strategy (PADS), a HK$126 billion (US$16.15 billion) project to enhance the "economic competitiveness" of Hong Kong. However, because the British government did not want to antagonize China, not only was the progress of PADS projects impeded but Wilson was recalled and lost his job. Similarly, the present governor, Chris Patten, sought to introduce moderate political reforms in Hong Kong to advance the pace of democratic development, earning him in the process the indignation of Beijing. Now his influence over Hong Kong policy has been diminished!

The Hong Kong government has also failed to make Legco more representative. The last Legco elections under British rule were held in September 1995. In this election, which were held under Patten's political reform package, 20 members were returned by direct elections by voters in geographical constituencies, 30 by functional constituencies and 10 by the Election Committee. This method to elect 60 Legco members was very unfair, for the 1.5 million homemakers, unemployed workers, retired elderly and full-time students who were above the age of 18 were limited to only one vote in their geographical constituency and deprived of a second vote in a functional constituency.

There is also an extraordinary imbalance in the number of voters that each legislator represents. For example, the new ninth constituency for public and community workers that was formed just prior to the 1995 election is huge with 2.7 million voters. These 2.7 million citizens have only one representative, but the Election Committee, composed of 283 district board members, can elect 10 Legco members! In addition, some of the old functional constituencies created prior to the 1995 election are extremely small, such as the functional constituencies for the

Urban Council and Regional Council with 39 and 37 members respectively. With such a small electorate, these elections are open to manipulation by interest groups. There were many alleged cases of corruption in the 1991 and 1995 elections, for instance, and one regional councillor was convicted of buying votes in the 1991 election and sentenced to three years in jail.

In order to have a truly representative government in Hong Kong, the governor, or the chief executive in the future SAR government, must be elected by the citizens of Hong Kong through universal franchise. Furthermore, all 60 members of Legco must also be returned by the most simple and fair way, namely, direct elections in geographical constituencies and on a one person, one vote basis.

Contrary to the views of some observers, it is incorrect to say that Hong Kong's people are disinterested in creating a fairer and more participatory governmental system in Hong Kong. Throughout the 1960s, especially after the riots in 1967, there were numerous pressure groups calling for political reforms in Hong Kong (in those days, government officials, especially the police, were corrupt); and in 1984, a group of 190 academics, professionals and clergymen called for an elected legislature in Hong Kong. The following year a coalition was formed at a rally held in November 1985 in the Ko Shan Theater calling for the introduction of direct elections in Legco in 1988. The rallies held in Victoria Park in the following three years echoed the same demand; but because of pressure from China, both the British and Hong Kong governments ignored their appeals. Finally, the international outcry over China's violent crackdown on the democratic movement in June 1989 as well as local demands for the right to vote forced Britain and China to agree to hold direct elections for Legco in September 1991.

Many people, both within and outside of Legco, continue to fight for more direct elections to the legislature, however. In July 1994, Emily Lau Wai-hing moved a private member's bill calling for all 60 members of Legco to be returned by direct elections. The bill was voted down by a margin of only one vote! Nevertheless, the quest for a fully representative government in Hong Kong continues.

With the rapid approach of 1997 - less than 500 days remain before the transfer of sovereignty - these efforts assume even more importance, especially with the changes announced by Beijing after power over Hong Kong is passed to them. Most worrisome are China's repeated statements that it will dismantle the present legislature in Hong Kong. Nowhere though does the Basic Law, Hong Kong's future mini-Constitution under the post-1997 SAR government, specify that the current Legco should be disbanded. On the contrary, the Basic Law assumes that those elected to Legco in 1995 will ride the "through train" and serve until their four-year term expires in 1999. That is why the Basic Law stipulates that the first Legco after 1997 will exist for only two years. This was explained even more clearly in the decision of the National People's Congress (NPC) on April 4, 1990, the date that the Basic Law was promulgated, when China's national legislative body determined the method in which the first government and legislature of the SAR would be formed. If China acts upon its threat to dismiss the Legco representatives elected by the people of Hong Kong in 1995, which no one doubts, it will be a serious reversal to Hong Kong's democratic movement.

In spite of its contributions described above, however, the Basic Law, which comes into effect on July 1, 1997, is a great hindrance to the democratic development of Hong Kong. It sets extremely stringent limits on the formation of Legco and the appointment of the chief executive; for according to the Basic Law, in the second term of Legco under the SAR government (1999-2003), 30 members will be returned by functional constituencies, six by the Election Committee and 24 by geographical constituencies. From 2003-2007 - the third term of Legco - the legislature will be formed by 30 members returned by functional constituencies and 30 by geographical constituencies. After the fourth term, Legco's composition will be decided by a review conducted before 2007.

The Basic Law also does not give the general populace of Hong Kong a voice on how the chief executive is chosen. According to the Basic Law, there will be a Selection Committee composed of 400 members established prior to 1997. Although they are all Hong Kong Chinese citizens, they are all appointed by the mainland. These 400 people will then recommend a candidate to officials in Beijing, who will make the official appointment.

It is not difficult to understand why the Basic Law contains so many deficiencies, for essentially it was drafted by a group of conservative Chinese officials and business tycoons from Hong Kong. It was also drafted at a time just after June 4, 1989, when China's top leaders were extremely nervous about the democratic movement in China. To them, democracy is synonymous with a threat to their authority and the toppling of their privileged position. As a result, they have tried to do everything possible to put the mainland, as well as Hong Kong, under their full control.

The democrats in Hong Kong need to convince China's leaders that democracy is not only good for Hong Kong but also for the mainland as well. The whole world is yearning for more democracy. It is futile for China's leaders to try to reverse this global trend. First, however, those desiring democracy in Hong Kong must try to allay the fears of local business leaders that democracy is bad for their business. The Democratic Party in Hong Kong, for example, chose the correct course by resisting the temptation to appease just the working class after its landslide victory in the 1995 Legco elections by taking into account the consequences of its proposals on the wider interests of the community.

There is no doubt though that the Basic Law retards the democratic development of Hong Kong. Concerned citizens in the territory must gather together and seek its amendment. The long-term democratic development of Hong Kong, however, depends a great deal on the next generation of local citizens. In order to equip them to be more responsible citizens (young people in Hong Kong are generally concerned with only making money), civic education, particularly democratic education, must be introduced in all secondary schools in Hong Kong immediately.

A TATTERED SOCIAL FABRIC

THE RICH GET RICHER

Hong Kong is a highly successful economic city. Its contributions as a financial and commercial center are well-appreciated by the international business community. *Fortune* magazine in October 1994 voted Hong Kong as the best city in the world to do business, and the World Economic Forum considered Hong Kong to be the third most competitive economy in the world, just after the United States and Singapore. Moreover, in its 1993 annual report, the secretariat of the General Agreement on Tariffs and Trade (GATT) listed Hong Kong as the eighth largest exporter and seventh largest importer in the world. In fact, its total exports for 1994 were US$160 billion, nearing Canada's US$164 billion and well ahead of China's US$130 billion.

Hong Kong also has the world's busiest container port. In 1995, it is estimated that Hong Kong handled a record 12.5 million teus (20-foot equivalent units). In addition, Hong Kong's airport handles more international flights daily than any other airport in the world.

Furthermore, *Asia Week* in its Feb. 2, 1996, issue reported that the per capita gross domestic product (purchasing power parity) in Hong Kong is US$22,527, considerably ahead of Britain (US$18,138) and Australia (US$19,007), surpassing even Japan (US$21,328) and Germany (US$20,165) and approaching the world leaders in this economic category, the United States (US$25,900) and Switzerland (US$24,483).

Yet this wealth in Hong Kong is unevenly distributed. In fact, it is highly concentrated with 5 percent of Hong Kong's population owning at least 80 percent of the city's total wealth. According to the *Hong Kong Economic Journal* in January 1996, the 10 richest families control more than half of the total value of the stock market in Hong Kong!

In a study about the gap between the rich and the poor in Hong Kong in 1993, a Baptist University lecturer discovered that a comparison between the 5 percent of the population in Hong Kong earning the highest salaries and the 5 percent earning the lowest indicated a difference of 12.5 times. It was 4.2 times in Taiwan and four times in Japan.

This disparity is evident by examining several local institutions. For example, a full professor in a university in Hong Kong earns about HK$100,000 (US$12,821) per month, plus housing and many fringe benefits, while a janitor in a university takes home only about HK$7,500 (US$962) per month. Likewise, the monthly income of the head of a government-subvented institution in Hong Kong now is more than HK$72,000 (US$9,231) per month; the figure for a young clerical assistant at the same institution is less than HK$7,000 (US$897) per month.

Over the past 20 years, despite Hong Kong's impressive economic success, the gap between the rich and the poor has continued to widen. In 1979, the gini-coefficient, an index measuring the gap between the rich and the poor ranging from 0 to 1, was 0.373. In 1991, it jumped to 0.476.

The major cause for this ever widening gap between the rich and the poor in Hong Kong is due to the fact that almost everything which people need is controlled by the rich: clothing, food, housing and public transportation. The 10 largest trading companies in Hong Kong, for instance, dominate the community's property market, public utilities and public transportation, all the way down to its retail businesses. Furthermore, for many years, Hong Kong's bank interest rates were determined by the Hong Kong Banking Association, and another association of publishers set the price of all Chinese daily newspapers. When the cartel rules, there is hardly fair and open competition. Consumers always lose.

The big companies, however, not only monopolize the essentials of people's livelihood, but they also shape the outcome of Hong Kong's important policy decisions. It is generally true to say that senior government officials make all of these decisions, or they try to create the illusion that they do, but Big Business heavily influences the government through its quiet lobbying, at least until 1991 when direct elections to the Legislative Council (Legco) allowed legislators with more concern for the people a seat in the legislature for the first time. Since then, the government has been forced to be more transparent and receptive to public demands.

Naturally though, since the wealthy play a major part in making public policies in Hong Kong, these policies greatly favor them. One example is the tax structure, which the Hong Kong government claims is the simplest and lowest in the world. The standard salaries tax is 15 percent, for instance. This is exceptionally low, especially in relation to tax rates in Europe and North America. Similarly, the profits tax is 17.5 percent. Asia's other three dragons should be envious of this, for the rate in Taiwan is 27 percent, 31 percent in Singapore and 34 percent in south Korea. Hong Kong's exceptionally low taxation rates though allow the rich to get even richer.

Another illustration indicating how the government's decisions favor the rich is its land policy. Since the government in general supports high land prices, the territory's developers have made full use of this policy to amass huge profits. A 500-square-foot apartment in a recently developed area in the New Territories, for instance, is worth HK$2 million (US$256,410); the average price for one square foot in a luxurious apartment in the Mid-Levels on Hong Kong Island is HK$8,000 (US$1,026). Moreover, as a rule, the market in Hong Kong uses gross floor area to describe the property rather than usable area, which is only 70 percent to 80 percent of the gross area.

The Poor Get Poorer

Life for the poor in Hong Kong has become even more difficult in the past three years, for Hong Kong has become one of the most expensive cities in the world in which to live. Inflation has been high for the last decade - an average of 8 percent to 11 percent per year. Consequently, many low-income people have experienced a negative wage increase. In 1994, wages for workers in Hong Kong's manufacturing sector actually decreased by an average of 2.9 percent while workers overall had a meager increase of just 0.4 percent.

In general, although wages for the past 25 years have increased 10 times, the cost of living has increased even faster. In 1970, for example, a daily newspaper cost 20 cents (US$0.03); now it costs HK$5 (US$0.64). In 1970, the cost of one square foot of land in Mongkok was about HK$100 (US$12.82); now it is HK$4,500 (US$577)! The living standard for a college graduate is much lower now than it was 25 years ago despite the fact that his or her salary has increased 10 times - a fact of life that is true for the majority of Hong Kong's residents.

Inflation, of course, is a major enemy of the poor in Hong Kong, yet the government has done little to reduce inflation. Almost every spring there is a price hike by the public utilities in the territory. This invariably has sparked an inflationary chain reaction. Hong Kong's public utilities are well-protected by the government though. They are allowed to make an annual profit of 15 percent. If they do not achieve this, they are permitted to increase their rates.

Generally, social services serve as an important means to balance the disparity in income between the rich and the poor. However, since the 1990s, the Hong Kong government has been extremely eager to recover the money they spend on social services. It has pushed very hard for the policy that citizens must pay according to their ability and the actual costs of the service. These two seemingly fair concepts are, in fact, disadvantageous to low-income people.

The government began the privatization process by establishing the Housing Authority a decade ago and the Hospital Authority in 1992. Since then, the three million people who live in public housing pay a great deal more than before. Furthermore, a patient who presently stays in a public hospital has to pay only HK$57 (US$7.31) per day; in 1997, it may be revised to HK$200 (US$25.64).

Moreover, despite Hong Kong's affluence, there is still no comprehensive social security system in Hong Kong. The government withdrew its proposal to establish the Old Age Pension Scheme (OAPS) in 1995. It now wishes to introduce a compulsory but privately managed provident fund. However, this plan will not help the unemployed and aged now; it will only benefit those who retire in 20 or 30 years.

The government insists that those who do not have any means by which to support themselves can apply for public assistance. Today, however, an elderly person who is a recipient of Comprehensive Social Security Assistance (CSSA) receives only about HK$60 (US$7.69) per day and is expected to survive on this meager allowance.

It is, thus, not surprising that the living conditions of the poor in Hong Kong remain appalling as well in the context described above. According to official figures, 156,900 citizens are living in temporary housing or as squatters, and 17,800 permanently reside on boats. This does not include street sleepers or those who stay in extremely poor private tenements. In addition, a pressure group in Hong Kong maintains that there are still 4,000 single men and women living in the "caged houses." (In a caged house apartment of 600 square feet, there may be 15 three-tiered bunk beds. Each person occupies one bunk, and a fence is built around it. Hence, the apartment looks like it is full of cages).

The government statistics released in 1995 reveal that 60.17 percent of the households in Hong Kong earn less than HK$10,000 per month (US$1,282), 37.74 percent are paid between HK$10,000 and HK$50,000 (US$1,282 and US$6,410), 1.68 percent take home a monthly salary of between HK$50,000 and HK$100,000 (US$6,410 and US$12,820) and 0.41 percent receive more than HK$100,000 (US$12,820) each month. This indicates that in Hong Kong today 60.17 percent of its citizens can barely survive and should be considered poor, 37.74 percent belong to the middle class, 1.68 percent are upper middle class and 0.41 percent should be classified as rich.

Moreover, the department of sociology at the University of Hong Kong did a survey in 1995 commissioned by Oxfam-Hong Kong. According to its findings, 230,000 households earn less than HK$4,000 (US$513) per month. The survey concluded that these families cannot escape the poverty trap. This disempowerment of the poor is disheartening for concerned people in Hong Kong.

In this economic environment, unemployment has created greater anxiety. According to several recent surveys, unemployment has overtaken housing, public transportation and even the changeover of sovereignty in 1997 to become the No. 1 concern of the people of Hong Kong. It is quite misleading to say that Hong Kong's unemployment rate of 3.6 percent reported in December 1995, an 11-year high, is low compared to the world's developed nations, for this figure must be put in context.

First, throughout the 1980s, unemployment in Hong Kong was almost non-existent. Even about two years ago Hong Kong's unemployment figure was only 2 percent. Thus, the recent rate represents a rather large increase in a short period of time.

Secondly, unemployment in Hong Kong is structural. Unemployment in the manufacturing sector has been very high due to the fact that many of the large factories in Hong Kong have moved their production lines to South China or to Southeast Asia. Even if we subscribe to the government's figures, there are now more than 110,000 unemployed people in Hong Kong, mostly middle-aged workers. The labor organizations, however, claim that the unemployment rate is as high as 7 percent, meaning that about twice this number of workers are without jobs. Statistics do not reveal the human dimensions of the problem though. The community was shocked in August 1995 when an unemployed worker committed suicide with his wife and 12-year-old daughter.

The government's actions, however, have not contributed to a solution to the unemployment challenges facing people in the territory. It was unwise for the government to introduce the General Labor Importation Scheme at the insistence of the business community in 1993. Under this program, 25,000 foreign workers have been hired to fill the vacancies resulting from the rapidly expanding service industry in Hong Kong. In addition to a thorough review of the labor importation scheme, the government should make every effort to derive ways to create jobs. It now has almost HK$300 billion (US$38.46 billion) in its reserves that it can use for this purpose.

In summary, the livelihood of the poor is becoming more and more difficult as Hong Kong becomes more and more affluent and expensive. This is true not only for the people of Hong Kong but for others who seek job opportunities in the territory as well. This includes the 148,000 women who work as domestic helpers and the more than 40,000 imported laborers who either are working on the new airport-related construction projects or under the General Labor Importation Scheme. In addition, the life of the approximately 19,000 Vietnamese asylum seekers who are confined in camps is also becoming more and more unbearable as the Chinese government as well as local residents become more impatient with their presence in Hong Kong.

A LESS CARING COMMUNITY

On the whole, the people of Hong Kong have become very self-centered. This in part is due to the impact of extreme materialism and secularism in the community and in part due to 1997, for what is certain about the uncertainties of 1997 is that most people believe that Hong Kong will enjoy fewer freedoms than it does today. This attitude is based on people's experiences as well as their perceptions because, first of all, almost half of the people in Hong Kong have migrated from the mainland. Since 1949, a great many of them have gone through endless political movements, notably the Great Leap Forward in 1958 and the Cultural Revolution from 1966 to 1976. These movements were extremely dehumanizing. Thousands of people lost their self-dignity if not their lives. Even China itself has made movies, like *Hibiscus Town*, to depict some of the human tragedies of these years. Deng Xiaoping and many Chinese leaders have assured the people, which includes the citizens of Hong Kong, that something like the Cultural Revolution will not happen again. After the violent crackdown of the pro-democracy movement in 1989, however, their assurances have been called into question.

In facing the future rule of the powerful communist regime in China, Hong Kong's citizens are now experiencing a sense of powerlessness. They have become extremely acquiescent. The silent majority has become very withdrawn, and the "everybody for themselves" mindset is predominant. Most people are now concentrating on working hard and making money. Many have even resorted to illegal means. Corruption in 1995, for instance, jumped 40 percent compared with the previous year. In order to make a few more dollars, several medical doctors were even caught selling illegal drugs to drug abusers or sick-leave or other medical certificates to patients. Moreover, many patients have complained that their doctors and dentists suddenly have begun charging exorbitant fees in recent months. Everyone in Hong Kong now wants to earn a few more fast dollars. Many have chosen gambling as their path to quick riches. The Jockey Club reported that the total turnover for the 1994-1995 horse racing year was HK$72 billion (US$9.23 billion), meaning on average every person in Hong Kong spent HK$12,000 (US$1,538) in legal gambling! In addition, many more have taken up illegal gambling, and hundreds of others play *mahjong* daily or weekly for money.

Working hard and making money are both stressful though. Hong Kong is now considered the world's most stressful city, which has given rise to many social as well as individual problems. One of the most serious problems in Hong Kong is that parents (many are single parents) are too busy earning money to give enough time to care for their children. One result is an alarming increase in the number of student suicides - almost one every two weeks in 1994.

For those who have earned a few dollars, many spend it on recreational activities (in order to release their tension, they claim). Consequently, certain restaurants and *karaoke* lounges continue to do well despite Hong Kong's recent economic downturn. Furthermore, people in Hong Kong drink more brandy than consumers in other parts of the world.

There are, of course, those who try to save enough money so that they can acquire an overseas passport. For those who want to immigrate to Canada, for instance, they must accumulate C$250,000 (US$179,856).

Because of this reaction to 1997, emigration is now a very serious problem in Hong Kong. Between 1984 and 1989, more than 100,000 citizens left permanently; and since 1989, almost 60,000 people have been part of the exodus every year. By 1997, almost one in 10 residents will have departed. The people who have emigrated are those with professional skills, experience and money. The resulting brain drain is an acute impediment to Hong Kong's development. For example, in the field of education, 20 principals of Hong Kong's 84 government schools have applied for early retirement in 1996, 22 stepped down in the summer of 1995 and 14 resigned in 1994.

The morale of Hong Kong's people is now low. If unchecked, Hong Kong society might disintegrate before the turn of the century. The current context has already led to bewildering responses to life. Days before the Mid-Autumn Festival in September 1995, for example, a merchant who makes mooncakes, a traditional food for this Chinese holiday, received a telephone call from a person claiming to be from the New China News Agency (NCNA). He told the merchant that Taiwan had been left off the map of China on the tin boxes in which the mooncakes were packaged. The merchant panicked. Without calling the NCNA to confirm its concern, he withdrew all of the boxes, illustrating the way in which China is making Hong Kong's citizens very nervous and irrational.

A Crisis in Education

Hong Kong's citizens are very pragmatic and profit-oriented. They have a very shallow value system which can best be described by two words: *immediate* and *tangible*. They want to make as much money as possible in the shortest period of time. Once they have their money, they spend it and have a good time. Helping others, job satisfaction, friendship, principles, etc., mean very little. This explains why so many "successful" business people have reversed their loyalties, from a pro-London stance a decade ago to a pro-Beijing point of view today. Yet very few of these "patriotic merchants" believe in what they say and do. They are just as afraid of communist rule as the general populace in Hong Kong. That is why most of them have secured a second passport, moved their families overseas and "diversified" their investments in other countries.

In reality, the mindset and behavior of Hong Kong's people described above has a great deal to do with the education system in the territory, for it is very much skills-oriented. It does not encourage students to think nor to raise questions. Students in Hong Kong are taught to obey authorities rather than guided to increase their analytical power. In recent years, both students' language abilities and their academic proficiency have slid from bad to worse; character formation in schools is practically absent. Concerned educators are very worried about a total collapse of the education system in Hong Kong in the near future.

In the past 40 years, although the government of Hong Kong has paid a great deal of attention to education, the bureaucrats in the Education Department have placed more emphasis on figures and numbers than on whether the young are really educated. As of 1978, for instance, Hong Kong has required nine years of compulsory education. Since the 1990s though, most of the financial resources for education have been put in the expansion of the tertiary sector. The governor in his fourth policy speech in October 1995 said that by 1997 a quarter of the relevant age group of students will be enrolled in a degree program. Quantity is good, but is quality still important? Every lecturer in the seven universities in Hong Kong complains about how horrendously low the standard is of his or her students. The only motivation of university students today is how to gain a degree so that they can secure a good job and earn lots of money. As a matter of fact, most of the university students have part-time jobs, and most of them carry a pager. In addition to these concerns about the educational system and the quality of present-day students, educators in Hong Kong think that it was a serious mistake for the government to reduce basic university education from four to three years.

There is something very wrong in the basic education program in Hong Kong as well; for despite the declining standard in students' (and teachers') language skills, the Education Department still is hesitant to force all high schools to use Chinese, the mother tongue of most of the students and teachers, as the medium of teaching.

To rectify the educational issues highlighted above, the government should put its valuable resources in the proper places, such as in ways to reduce the number of students in each class (perhaps 30 in high schools and 35 in primary schools), to change all dual-session primary schools in which students only attend school half a day into full-day schools and to directly subsidize all kindergartens so that the quality of these teachers can be greatly improved.

In addition, more resources must be made available for training teachers at all levels. Students do learn by the examples they encounter in life and in the classroom, yet the manners, character and commitment of most of the teachers in Hong Kong nowadays are far from desirable. An overhaul of the whole educational system in the territory is long overdue. The place of entry may very well be the re-education of all those who seek to be teachers of Hong Kong's youth. They must learn that they are embarking on a career path to serve a profession to prepare and mold the future of the community, not merely to make a living.

SILENT PROPHETS AND LOST SHEEP

PRO-ESTABLISHMENT

The British brought many things to the colony of Hong Kong. One was Christianity; another was a close church-state relationship. Although unlike England where the king or queen is the head of the church and many of the bishops from the Church of England sit in the House of Lords, the two bishops in Hong Kong, nevertheless, occupy important positions. The official protocol list places the Anglican bishop and the Roman Catholic cardinal at the fourth and fifth highest positions, just behind the commander of the British armed forces, the chief secretary and the chief justice - a reflection of the tremendous influence and privileges that both churches enjoy in the colony.

Soon after the acquisition of Hong Kong by the British, many missionary societies arrived in the territory. In addition to establishing places of worship, many opened schools as well. Thirty or 40 years ago, of the 30 most famous secondary schools, 25 were operated by the missionary societies, such as the London Missionary Society, the Church Missionary Society, the Jesuits, Maryknolls and several other Roman Catholic orders (the other five were directly run by the government). Many of today's senior civil servants, successful professionals, businessmen and businesswomen went to these "elitist" schools. Consequently, the churches in Hong Kong have indirectly helped to consolidate the territory's elitist social system. As a result, the leadership of the traditional denominations and local congregations is extremely pro-establishment.

In real terms, the Christian Church in Hong Kong only began to develop in the 1950s. Before the Communists took control of mainland China, most missionary societies considered Hong Kong to be simply a stepping stone to China as their work was concentrated on the mainland. Hong Kong was treated as primarily a place of rest and recreation for their missionaries.

The change of government in China in 1949, however, altered this perception drastically. Many foreign missionary societies were forced to leave China. Part of their human as well as material resources came to Hong Kong because by the early 1950s Hong Kong had become a center for hundreds of refugees who were fleeing China daily.

In the 1960s, when Hong Kong began to develop economically, its churches shifted their focus from relief work to providing formal education to thousands of children. A pattern of partnership was formed between the government and the denominational churches. The former provided the land and money while the latter assumed full responsibility for building and managing the community's schools. Without the churches' involvement, children in Hong Kong would not have enjoyed nine years of compulsory education since 1978. Later this partnership was extended to the provision of social welfare and health care. The churches in Hong Kong, for example, have helped to initiate a number of innovative social programs and services to combat the social as well as human problems of the 1970s. Their efforts have been well-appreciated by the wider community. Today churches in Hong Kong are responsible for more than 60 percent of the social welfare work undertaken in the community, operate more than 40 percent of the city's schools and administer about 20 percent of its hospitals.

But the Christian Church in Hong Kong is a victim of its success. The management of such a big service empire has absorbed the energy of its best people. Church leaders spend much of their time attending meetings. They can hardly spare any time to read, do social analysis and reflect on what is happening theologically in the life of the community and the world.

Furthermore, since the denominational leaders have to rely heavily on the government and the wealthy to support their work, they are not free to challenge the ways in which the wealthy and government are using the masses for their own benefit. Emily Lau Wai-hing, a popular elected legislator, described this unusual relationship as "The Unholy Alliance." Consequently, because church leaders in Hong Kong are very much a part of the establishment, they are not in favor of challenging the status quo. Occasionally, however, there have been young pastors who have decided to fight for social justice or to challenge the decisions of those in authority. Eventually they were advised by their supervisors to stay away from "controversial" issues or were totally silenced. One young priest was advised by his bishop to take a study leave after he raised questions about the establishment inside and outside of the Church. He lamented later that his church actually follows 11 commandments. The 11th commandment reads: "Don't rock the boat; play it safe."

UN-CHRISTIAN CHRISTIANS

A Christian is a disciple of Christ. He or she should learn from and follow what Jesus Christ said and did. According to Matthew's Gospel, Jesus was constantly busy, serving not Himself but others: "He went about all the cities and villages, teaching, preaching and healing . . ." (cf. Matt. 4:23 and 9:35). Dietrich Bonhoffer summed this up neatly: "Jesus was 'a man for others.'" In addition, the most famous hymn about Christ as found in Phil. 2:6-11 described Jesus in the following way: "Jesus was in the same position as God, but He gave it up and came to this world as a slave. For the sake of humankind, He gave up His life on a cross (the most humiliating way to die) and was buried." The Apostles Creed adds that "He descended into hell." Jesus's own self-understanding, according to the Synoptic Gospels, was that "the Son of Man came not to be served but to serve and to give His life as a ransom for many" (Mark 10:45). From the highest to the lowest, Jesus, thus, emptied Himself so that people's lives could be filled.

Today as we look around Hong Kong most Christians are only interested in having their lives filled. In fact, they are quite prepared to allow or even to ask those in need to sacrifice for them!

Oftentimes church leaders and pastors in Hong Kong have set poor examples for Christians to live a Christ-like life. They are too status- and benefits-oriented. Pastors act more like senior officials than ministers (the word *minister* literally means "to give service to"), for pastors today are far too busy managing schools, social centers, etc. They have little or no time to teach, to preach the Word of God, to counsel and support their parishioners. For the few pastors who take the teaching ministry more seriously, they are frequently not prepared to confront their parishioners with the harsh realities and the moral dilemmas that they face in their daily life. Few dare to challenge what their parishioners do. Most of the pastors want to be popular and, therefore, are too often too willing to only say things pleasing to their parishioners.

As a result, most of the Christians today do not find that the Christian faith really can help them face the challenges or crises that they face. This explains why the departure rate for Christians in the past decade is more than double that for the overall population in Hong Kong.

The above descriptions are primarily about the phenomena and activities of the mainline churches in Hong Kong, which have a total membership of 250,000 in the Roman Catholic Church and approximately 80,000 in the Anglican and other major Protestant denominations. Altogether they worship in about 400 parish churches and parish centers.

As for the evangelical wing of the Christian Church in Hong Kong, it has more than 130,000 members. They belong to about 800 local congregations which, in turn, support almost 200 parachurch organizations whose major functions are to evangelize the residents of Hong Kong as well as the people on the mainland and overseas Chinese.

The teachings of the evangelical churches are usually extremely conservative and inward looking. Their members are required to follow countless "thou shall nots" taken literally from the Bible. These moral precepts are so devoid of the realities of modern-day life that even pastors and teachers from time to time find them difficult to follow. Many of the older members have unconsciously fallen into living a life based on double standards, being a devout church leader on Sundays in church but between Mondays and Saturdays leading a lifestyle that is no different from most non-Christians, playing *mahjong* and betting on horse races, conducting business deals under the table, etc. With these kinds of examples set by older Christians, many young fundamentalist Christians have split personalities as a result.

Christianity, however, cannot be defined by a set of morals or even beliefs. The Christian faith calls people to be faithful to Jesus, who intensely lived His life within His social context, trying to help others to live a fuller life. Christians, therefore, must take their own life experiences and those of others more seriously. The dualistic way to look at this world, as the traditional churches do, is far from adequate. God so loved this world that Jesus came into this world and lived for this world, thus, so must the Church.

Undoubtedly, the teachings of the conservative and evangelical churches in Hong Kong have rendered their churches quite irrelevant to the whole social process. This contributes to the silence of the Church in Hong Kong in this crucial period of Hong Kong's history.

Religious Freedom

Christians all over the world are deeply worried about religious freedom. This is especially true for Hong Kong's Christians as they approach 1997, for the persecution of Christians in China did not take place only during the Cultural Revolution from 1966 to 1976 when all churches were closed and their buildings occupied: it still continues today. The possibility of such a response by the government in Hong Kong after 1997 is very real.

Whenever the question of religious freedom in Hong Kong after 1997 has been raised, Chinese officials have always replied by saying that it is guaranteed in the Basic Law, which states in Article 32: "Hong Kong residents shall have freedom of conscience. Hong Kong residents shall have freedom of religious belief and freedom to preach and to conduct and participate in religious activities in public."

This has not set the hearts of concerned Christians in the territory at rest. As is widely known, the Basic Law, as well as all other laws, are subject to interpretation. Unfortunately, China has reserved this right for the Standing Committee of the National People's Congress (NPC) in Beijing rather than for the Court of Final Appeal (CFA) in Hong Kong, a body that is more appropriately suited for this role given the fact that the Joint Declaration stipulates that the Hong Kong Special Administrative Region (SAR) will enjoy a highly autonomous status.

The enforcement of any law is also subject to the understanding of the "enforcers." Chinese officials, by and large, do not understand the meaning of religion, much less religious freedom. In Hong Kong, for example, Christian activists believe that the Church, as a prophet, should speak out on public issues which affect the livelihood of the masses. However, Chinese officials certainly do not consider it proper for the Church to criticize the government.

Denominational leaders who are concerned about the continuation of their social service empire after 1997 are quite satisfied about the guarantee given to them in the Basic Law (cf. Article 141). As a matter of fact, the Anglican bishop and several Anglican businessmen who served on the Basic Law Drafting Committee ensured that such provisions were included in the Basic Law.

However, the truth of the matter is that in a totalitarian regime everything is judged by its value. If the Christian Church in Hong Kong is useful to the government, it will be given more space to speak and to act; if it threatens or makes the government uncomfortable, it will be suppressed. This offers another reason why church leaders in Hong Kong admonish their members to remain quiet.

For those who are genuinely concerned about religious freedom, however, they must view it from a much wider perspective. Religious freedom is only possible when there is freedom of expression, freedom of assembly and especially freedom of the press. In China, many Christians have been arrested because they have conducted their religious activities in non-registered places (in China, strictly speaking, there is no freedom of assembly). Moreover, Christians in rural areas, where reporting by the press is difficult, are harassed by Public Security Bureau (PSB) officials more so than in large cities. Thus, in fighting for the preservation of religious freedom, concerned Christians and others must also not forget the importance of the safeguarding of other forms of basic human rights.

However, this is not enough, for those who are committed to upholding human rights must also be dedicated to fostering and strengthening democracy. Only a democratically responsible government is motivated to safeguard its citizens' basic freedoms. Although Hong Kong is not likely to have a fully elected government in the foreseeable future (meaning its citizens are able to elect their own chief executive and all 60 legislators by universal franchise), a more open and accountable government must be pursued.

Finally, Hong Kong will not become an independent nation in 1997 (no one in Hong Kong advocates such a vision); it will be a part of China. Consequently, Hong Kong and China will be closely linked. If Hong Kong is not doing well, it will become a huge liability to China. Likewise, if there is no genuine political reform in China, any democracy in Hong Kong will be short-lived. Thus, Hong Kong's citizens, as well as those who are concerned about Hong Kong, must try to contribute to China's development, not only economically, but politically as well.

CHURCH REFORM

The powerful, traditional and conservative Roman Catholic Church in its ecumenical council from 1962 to 1964, Vatican II, used "Aggioramento" (Updating) as its theme. The Christian Church in Hong Kong needs to adopt the same theme as it faces the challenges presented by 1997. Like the Presbyterian motto "Ecclesia Reformanda Semper Reformata" (The Church Renews, Ever Renewing), the Church in Hong Kong needs to be reformed, both in its structure as well as in its mission. First, it has to unburden itself from its enormous ecclesiastical and social institutions. The Church in Hong Kong was a social pioneer in the 1960s and 1970s. It introduced many new social services to address the tremendous social as well as human needs of those decades. Now the government and the community are ready to shoulder this social responsibility. Consequently, the Church can move on to new terrain.

For too long, the Church in Hong Kong has ignored public issues which affect the livelihood of the masses. It must be made clear that the Church exists for the poor, the powerless and those who need special care. It must be in solidarity with these people and be sensitive to their needs. In a society tipped toward one side, i.e., for and by the rich and the powerful, the Church needs to do a great deal of "balancing."

The Church in Hong Kong must relearn how to confront the rich and the powerful, for the powerful Chinese regime will assume responsibility for Hong Kong in 1997. Like any other regime, it will use "divide and rule" tactics. In 1995, for example, the New China News Agency (NCNA) organized a meeting for the heads of the seminaries in Hong Kong. Reportedly, the head of one who is considered to be "unfriendly" to the Church in China was not invited. Moreover, in 1994, the Hong Kong Women Christian Council (HKWCC) sponsored a conference for Chinese women theologians from Taiwan, China and Hong Kong. The representatives from China, who were eager to attend, could not get permission to leave the country though. According to one source in China, since HKWCC was considered a pressure group that was critical of the government on the mainland, China could not let their citizens be exposed to their views.

Certainly China is applying a great deal of both direct and indirect pressure on church leaders and Christians in Hong Kong. Many have turned their allegiance to China without careful consideration; many church leaders have intentionally isolated their own brothers and sisters. For instance, a seminary decided not to reinvite a part-time lecturer to teach in 1995 because of a telephone call from the NCNA.

The Church in Hong Kong must try to prevent what happened at the Last Supper: Jesus's prediction that one of His disciples was going to betray Him as recorded in Chapter 13 of the Gospel of John. Indeed, the Church in Hong Kong must work to ensure that what happened time and time again in Eastern Europe, the Soviet Union and China will not happen in Hong Kong now or after 1997. The churches and Christians in Hong Kong must come together. They must stop seeking benefits for themselves and their own "salvation" under Chinese rule and instead start to live for others, like Jesus. As a whole, the Church in Hong Kong must maintain a distance from the rich and the powerful. On behalf of all of Hong Kong's citizens, the Church must be a watchdog over the activities of the rich and powerful by maintaining a critical stance toward their endeavors.

In addition to this role, theological education in Hong Kong needs to be improved. The churches in Hong Kong should make theological education their highest priority. By one estimation, only about 1 percent of the total offerings received by the Church (i.e., about HK$10 million [US$1.28 million]) are budgeted to support the 18 seminaries and Bible schools in the territory, which are the product of overseas missionary societies from the West. Thus, Hong Kong's churches do not lack financial resources. Moreover, the Council for World Mission or CWM (the former London Missionary Society) sold a hospital site in 1994 for HK$1.63 billion (about US$209 million), and the American Baptists sold six properties in Kowloon Tong, an expensive residential area, for almost HK$462 million (US$59.23 million). More of these financial resources should be put into theological education; for in geographical terms, Hong Kong is a small place. It is asking far too much of the churches in Hong Kong to support the same number of seminaries as found in Australia and Aotearoa (New Zealand) combined. The 18 seminaries and Bible schools, thus, should make efforts for closer cooperation and even possible mergers. This is the only way to survive more meaningfully. This is also the only way to upgrade the quality of theological education in Hong Kong.

There are other related issues in the field of theological education in the territory that necessitate action as well. Seminaries in Hong Kong have an awesome task ahead as Christians in Hong Kong in general are extremely poorly educated theologically and their pastors are inadequately equipped. First, however, they must re-examine their curriculum, for typically, the curriculum of any seminary in Hong Kong is no different than those of the seminaries in the West 20 or 30 years ago. They are outdated and directed towards a social and cultural context which is irrelevant to Hong Kong. Consequently, the territory's seminaries must reformulate the content of theological education in Hong Kong on the local context of both today and tomorrow.

Theological education in Hong Kong also faces other challenges, for seminaries in Hong Kong, by and large, are supported by local churches, although, as noted above, in a very limited fashion. Thus, seminaries always want to build a better relationship with the local churches. Oftentimes they do this at the expense of their principles. It is not surprising that seminaries in Hong Kong produce a great many obedient "servants" for local churches. These locally educated pastors though are not equipped to discharge their role of leading their congregations to be more open and more Christ-like. God, however, prefers to be worshiped through acts of justice rather than through acts of piety. Therefore, let the following be the dictum of those who engage in theological education:

"I reject your oblations
And refuse to look at your sacrifices of fattened cattle.
Let me have no more the din of your chanting,
No more of your strumming on harps.
But let justice flow like water
And integrity like an unfailing stream." (Amos 5:22-24)

VOCAL CHOPSTICKS AND INTERNATIONAL SOLIDARITY

PEOPLE'S VOICES

Generally speaking, Hong Kong's citizens are apathetic. They are afraid to speak up for fear of unknowingly offending the authorities. In China, if you offend those in authority, eventually they will find you again, and then you will face the dire consequences. This is known as the "settling of accounts."

On the mainland, things can best be done if you know those in authority and can get clearance or support from them. Business people in China spend a lot of valuable time wining and dining those with power to establish and maintain good relationships or *guanxi* with government officials or with those who are influential. Based on this, Western experts on China invariably advise Hong Kong's citizens to pay more respect, "to give face," to Chinese officials. In return, they will be kind to Hong Kong.

As this world is about to enter the 21st century, however, no one should live in fear for their safety. People all over the world yearn for a more open and free society. Only if the rule of law prevails will such a society come about. Hence, the rule of law is not only good for the people on the street, but it is even more important for those in business. The rule of law guarantees fair competition and good business rather than rule by *guanxi*.

However, the rule of law has to be backed by a free press and an open and accountable government. Hong Kong's citizens must speak up and demand that these be initiated and implemented sooner rather than later.

In the elections in September 1995, more than 920,000 citizens in Hong Kong spoke up in the voting booth. Most of them wanted to elect their representatives to the Legislative Council (Legco), which is a body to monitor the performance of the Hong Kong government and ensure that it is responsive and accountable to the citizens of Hong Kong.

It has often been argued that Hong Kong's citizens are more interested in their meal ticket (job) than their ballot (voting rights), but gradually, they have come to know that both are equally important. Without a semielected legislature in Hong Kong in recent years, the government certainly would have continued the General Labor Importation Scheme that grants 25,000 overseas laborers work in the service industries as well as on small construction projects. This, in turn, would throw thousands of local laborers out of work.

Those in authority do not generally give up their power and privileges easily. The power of the rulers and civil liberties are always in opposition. The rulers want to set limits on citizens' rights - the narrower, the better - while most citizens insist that government officials should not be given excessive powers. Thus, concerned citizens must always fight for a wider scope of freedoms for ordinary people rather than for only those few who enjoy wealth. People must be encouraged to adopt a "contending spirit" so that their civil liberties cannot be taken away easily by government officials. In the broadest context, freedoms and other civil liberties, such as basic human rights, are inborn. People do not need to *kowtow* or bend to government authorities in order to enjoy their rights.

Human nature is frail. Power can corrupt people very easily. Consequently, all powers must be checked. Furthermore, as human beings, all people - officials included - are prone to err.

Thus, Hong Kong's citizens must maintain a critical stance toward all senior government officials.

A deputy director of the New China News Agency (NCNA) once complained to the press that he did not understand why the Hong Kong government would allow Han Dongfang, a Chinese labor leader, to stay in the territory. The fact of the matter is that Han was given a Chinese passport to go to the United States for medical treatment after he was released from prison after being sentenced for his efforts to form an independent trade union in China during the Tiananmen Square protests in 1989. On his return to China in 1993, he was ousted from his hotel room in Guangzhou in southern China and deported to Hong Kong by security officers. Not only was he denied entry to his own country, but his passport was confiscated by the Chinese border officials. Effectively, Han became stateless. If Hong Kong refused to allow him to stay, where would he go? Hong Kong's citizens must be brave enough to speak the truth. "Speaking up" can counteract lies which rulers consistently use to justify their actions and policies.

Lee Kuan-yew, former prime minister of Singapore, and Percy Craddock, former British ambassador to China, often advise the people of Hong Kong not to confront the Chinese authorities, but the fact is that Hong Kong cannot confront China, a very powerful country with one of the world's largest militaries. Moreover, the mainland's population is two hundred times larger than that of Hong Kong, and its geographical size dwarfs Hong Kong by 10,000 times. In spite of this, Hong Kong's people must speak up for themselves. Otherwise, the Chinese leaders may not know the realities of Hong Kong - what makes Hong Kong successful and what is best for the territory. Hong Kong's citizens are in favor of rejoining the motherland of China, but they have many misgivings about communist rule.

Local Chinese advisors in Hong Kong have advised their fellow citizens to be less confrontational with the mainland and to have more dialogue with its officials, but unfortunately China has decided to have discussions with only a very small group of people in Hong Kong, namely, those who speak the same language (at least openly) as China's leaders. Beijing has yet to show its sincerity that it wants to listen to the views of Hong Kong's people from all walks of life. China, for instance, refused to listen to more than 1.1 million citizens who, through a signature campaign in 1986, asked the Chinese government to abandon its plan to build a nuclear power plant in Daya Bay, 50 kilometers from Hong Kong. It refused as well to heed the call from millions of citizens, including its own cadres assigned to Hong Kong, that it should refrain from sending troops into Tiananmen Square in the spring of 1989. China also totally disregarded a plea from Hong Kong's journalists and many human rights groups to release Xi Yang, a Hong Kong reporter who accidentally stumbled onto a story in 1994 about future changes in China's interest rates - something which the Chinese authorities forbid to be independently disclosed - which subsequently led to Xi being sentenced to 12 years in prison.

Hong Kong's people must speak up. They cannot rely on the representatives appointed by the Chinese authorities to speak on their behalf; for instead of reflecting the worries and wishes of Hong Kong's citizens, these advisors only reflect what the mainland leaders want to hear. Reportedly, many of the local Chinese advisors in Hong Kong privately confide to their relatives and friends that even they do not believe the things they say in public; but in order to please the government and party officials in Beijing, they have to continue acting. This is why the Preliminary Working Committee's (PWC) subgroup on legal affairs proposed to reinstate six laws that were invalidated because they contravened the Bill of Rights. They know that human rights is a taboo concept for China's leaders. Therefore, anything they do to curtail citizens' human rights in Hong Kong, even if it means to reverse the gains that have been made in the community, is desirable.

Meanwhile, the business community is very quietly manipulating government officials in Hong Kong to believe in what they say and what they propose. As a result, the territory's citizens have to engage in serious dialogue with the business community. Hong Kong's citizens are not anti-business; they only want a fairer share of the fruits which the territory's economic success has produced. No one in Hong Kong wants to live on welfare as the business people claim. Quite the contrary, Hong Kong's people in general want to be self-reliant. The business people in Hong Kong ought to realize that a successful economy and social benefits are not mutually exclusive. Likewise, democracy is good for business, for it advocates a fuller participation of all segments of society. It also engenders a genuine sense of belonging. In the final analysis, genuine economic development not only means a growth in productivity (the forecast for the growth of Hong Kong's gross domestic product [GDP] is 5 percent for 1995, 1996 and 1997), but equally important, it includes a more even distribution of the wealth generated (Hong Kong is exceptionally poor in this regard).

If the people of Hong Kong ask China not to interfere in the territory's affairs, they are merely asking Beijing to keep its promises that are enshrined in the Joint Declaration of 1984. As Hong Kong continues to develop, it needs its economic system to remain intact and an independent government constituted by representatives elected by all of Hong Kong's citizens. This is what the Joint Declaration means when it guarantees "one country, two systems," "Hong Kong people governing Hong Kong" and "the government of the Special Administrative Region (SAR) having an autonomous status."

Hong Kong has reached a very critical period. In order to go forward, the citizens of Hong Kong must play a more active role. The right to express their views and feelings is of utmost importance. Hong Kong's people must look beyond their own interests and self-preservation and must stand together. A pair of chopsticks can be broken easily, but it is extremely difficult for anyone to break five pairs of chopsticks grouped together.

Changes in China

Overall, in the past 47 years, China has progressed remarkably well. It has become a powerful country. Its economy is the third largest in the world, just after the United States and Japan. For the first time in decades, no one must go hungry. Despite the many setbacks during the various political movements between the 1950s and 1970s, China in general has taken many steps forward, although as one China watcher has observed, every time China has gone two paces forward, it soon moves one pace backward.

Since 1979, China has taken many important strides forward though. First, under Deng Xiaoping, China decided to reopen its doors to the international community. More importantly, however, it has given up its rigid planned economy.

There have also been important moves within the country for political reform. Under Qiao Shi, for instance, the National People's Congress (NPC) has become more assertive. It wants to scrutinize more closely the ruling party's policies and important appointments. In 1995 when Premier Li Peng asked the NPC to endorse his proposal to create positions for two new vice premiers and nominated Wu Bangguo and Jiang Chunyun to fill these posts, there was an exceptionally large number of NPC delegates who voted against these proposals or abstained. Gradually, the NPC refuses to be a rubber stamp. Furthermore, the Chinese People's Political Consultative Conference (CPPCC) under Li Ruihuan has become more independent and alive in recent years as well.

China needs to intensify its efforts in political as well as economic reform though. Totalitarian rule is outdated. In a pluralistic society, people are bound to hold different views. Governments throughout the world - China included - must learn to appreciate not only dissenting views but especially to learn from criticism directed towards their policies and programs.

Before the military junta came to power in the 1960s, for example, Burma was a rice-exporting country. Now Burma is one of the poorest nations in Asia. Similarly, in the early 1950s, the differences in living standards in Hong Kong, Taiwan and China were minimal. Now the per capita GDP (purchasing power parity or ppp) for Hong Kong is US$22,527 while it is US$13,235 for Taiwan and as low as US$2,660 for China (cf. the Feb. 2, 1996, issue of *Asia Week*). One of the primary reasons is that Hong Kong's citizens are given much more room to maneuver than those in Taiwan who, likewise, have much more freedom to operate than those in China. China's own experiments with the creation of the special economic zones (SEZs) in 1980 also demonstrate the same point. For instance, in terms of economic development, Shenzhen, the first SEZ in China, is almost approaching the level of Hong Kong.

Another important area which China is now working on earnestly is the overhaul of its legal system. The highly publicized Qing Dao Lake case in 1994 (first the local authorities insisted there was only an accidental fire on a pleasure boat containing Taiwanese tourists on the lake; later, after the public outcry in Taiwan, they admitted that it was a robbery and arson case, leading to the arrest, trial and execution of three robbers within days) and the treatment of an Australian-Chinese merchant, James Peng Jiandong, (Peng was kidnaped in Macau in October 1993, brought to China and kept in a secret location for a year, long enough for the Chinese authorities to amend the company law to convict him) indicate that China must still undertake many important changes to reform its legal system and to make its law enforcement agencies more responsible and accountable.

China is certainly going to change though. Jiang Zemin and his close comrades know very well that they lack the prestige and the authority of Mao Zedong, Deng Xiaoping and the other elder statesmen who helped to shape the Chinese Communist Party (CCP) during the Long March in 1934 and who brought forth modern China in 1949. Therefore, in order to rule the most populous nation in the world, they have to rely on the support of the military as well as its 1.2 billion people. However, the people are not about to give China's leaders their unconditional support unless their demands for a higher standard of living and more freedoms are met. Consequently, Jiang and other leaders have boosted reforms economically and politically while Deng, their mentor, is still living.

Meanwhile, the more liberal the Chinese leaders are, the better for Hong Kong. China must adopt a "let go and let live" attitude towards Hong Kong. That is the only way for Hong Kong to prosper further. Any interference from China can jeopardize Hong Kong's development. As Fanny Wong, a political commentator, said, "Why change a system that works?"

Undoubtedly, China does not want to inhibit Hong Kong's growth, for Hong Kong is useful to the mainland. Hong Kong serves as an engine for China's development. Hong Kong acts as a bridge between China and the rest of the world. Hong Kong can export its valuable experience regarding a free economy, financial management, the rule of law and various freedoms to China. Hong Kong's citizens are patriotic. They want to contribute to China in whatever way they can. Beijing must trust the citizens of Hong Kong who have no quarrel with Chinese sovereignty. Hong Kong's people are only afraid of Beijing's interference in the affairs of their community.

China, in addition, wants Hong Kong to do well for other reasons. One pertains to its national pride. If Britain can make Hong Kong stable and prosperous, so can China. The mainland also desperately wants to fully participate in the international community as a key player. China is eager to exhibit its competence to its chief adversary - the United States - and its key trade partners - the European Union (EU) and Japan - as well as many of the Third World countries who look up to China.

China also wants to make the "one country, two systems" experiment in Hong Kong a success. That is the only way it can peacefully coax Taiwan to return to the motherland at the beginning of the next century.

THE INTERNATIONAL COMMUNITY'S SUPPORT

For China, the way it will manage Hong Kong is a domestic affair. Its leaders believe that they have the right to govern Hong Kong in whatever way they see fit; foreigners should not become involved. This is why China was angry at Chris Patten, Hong Kong's last British governor, when he solicited support for his blueprint for political reforms in Hong Kong from the United States, Canada, Japan and Australia and was warmly received by the heads of these governments. For this, Patten was dubbed an "international prostitute" by Beijing.

China has repeatedly warned against the internationalization of the Hong Kong issue. This is why Beijing went against the provisions of the Basic Law, Hong Kong's future mini-Constitution, and allowed no more than one expatriate judge to sit on the Court of Final Appeal (CFA), the highest court in Hong Kong after 1997, and why it will move to ban all local political organizations from having any overseas links after 1997.

However, Hong Kong is an international city. Close to 400,000 expatriates from all over the world are living, working or studying in Hong Kong. Moreover, in 1995, 12 million tourists, who spent HK$75 billion (US$9.62 billion), visited the territory. In addition, more than 4,000 overseas incorporated companies as well as many other companies owned and controlled by foreign interests are now in Hong Kong. Naturally, the international business community continues to maintain a close watch on Hong Kong. They are keen to see that the rights of individuals as well as the rights of their companies in Hong Kong are safeguarded. They know this is only possible if Hong Kong's rule of law administered by an independent and impartial judiciary as well as an open and minimalist government remain intact after 1997. Thus, when Sir Leon Brittan, the EU's trade commissioner, in July 1995 issued a call for democratic reform in China and when Warren Christopher, the U.S. secretary of state, urged China to respect Hong Kong's elected legislature, they were not idly speaking without any support. The international business community is fully aware that fair competition in China and in Hong Kong is only possible if there is the rule of law backed by a democratic government.

In the case of Hong Kong, China has promised not to interfere in matters concerning the territory with the exception of defense and foreign affairs. These are enshrined in the Sino-British Joint Declaration, an agreement signed between the present and future sovereign governments in December 1984, which has been tabled at the United Nations. As an international agreement, the international community and the United Nations have every right to ensure that both China and Britain honor it in both letter and spirit.

The Joint Declaration and the Basic Law also state that the two international covenants on human rights will remain in force in Hong Kong after 1997. As the body entrusted to oversee how the International Covenant on Civil and Political Rights (ICCPR) and the International Covenant on Economic, Social and Cultural Rights (ICESCR) are applied, it is reasonable for the United Nations Human Rights Commission to require a periodic report about Hong Kong from its sovereign government, even though China is not yet a signatory of these two covenants.

Other international non-governmental organizations (NGOs) and the ecumenical church who are interested in the continuation of the rule of law in Hong Kong after 1997 and in maintaining a respect for human rights, such as the International Commission of Jurists (ICJ) and the World Council of Churches (WCC), must keep a close watch over Hong Kong after the transfer of its sovereignty. It must be underlined that the advocacy of democracy and human rights are not a posture that is synonymous with being anti-China. Rather, it is a win-win situation. If Hong Kong continues to thrive, it will bring immense benefits to China and, indeed, to the rest of the international community and global marketplace, for the whole world is moving towards a more open and civil society, a less closed and state-controlled global context. No one should be allowed to reverse this trend.

It seems that Hong Kong's future prospects as a free economy and a free society are declining if recent local surveys revealing such a trend are accurate. Prudence indicates that it would be wise for people abroad as well as Hong Kong's citizens to heed these signs. Now many people from all over the world are concerned about the state of affairs in Tibet. The Chinese government and the Tibetan government signed a pact in May 1951 whose contents are very similar to the Sino-British Joint Declaration outlining Hong Kong's future. The international community paid no attention to Tibet though until 1989 when the Dalai Lama, the spiritual leader of Tibet, was awarded the Nobel Peace Prize. By then, however, it was too late to improve on conditions in Tibet as China had ruled it with an iron fist for almost 40 years. Therefore, the international community must begin monitoring developments in Hong Kong immediately.

In the next 500 days, many things can happen in Hong Kong that may have serious ramifications. If China follows through with its threats, the 3,000 non-ethnic Chinese people who were born and grew up in Hong Kong will not be given SAR passports and will consequently become "stateless." The destiny of the approximately 19,000 Vietnamese boat people is uncertain as well. Furthermore, the present Legco will be dismantled, and outspoken democratic leaders, like Martin Lee Chu-ming, Emily Lau Wai-hing and Szeto Wah, will be barred from participating in any future elections despite the fact that they were elected with the highest number of votes in both the 1991 and 1995 Legco elections. It would be a grave mistake if people think that these individuals are expendable and, therefore, accept the fate which is sealed for them; for if the authorities can rid themselves of the people they do not like so easily, sooner or later the same fate will befall anyone which is offensive to them. This was the case in many of the Eastern European countries before 1989. If China can dismiss Legco today and dilute the Bill of Rights tomorrow without any protest, eventually Hong Kong's rule of law and its entire system will disappear!

There are a great many citizens in Hong Kong who are fighting to have the Hong Kong system and way of life preserved or even improved. The international community should stand alongside them. When the European Parliament voted in 1994 to allocate HK$1.8 million (US$230,769) to assist human rights education and advocacy in Hong Kong, it was an important symbol of solidarity; it was a big boast for the morale of the advocates of democracy in Hong Kong.

We are now living in a global society. The struggle in Hong Kong is a struggle for others as well. The international community and the people of Hong Kong should stand together in this chapter of Hong Kong's history. As long as people do not give up, the impossible will become possible.

In summary, this book has attempted to tell the story of Hong Kong. The territory has gone through difficult periods many times before; but because of its citizens' resilience and hard work and the attention and care given by the international community, Hong Kong went from strength to strength. An economic miracle was brought forth in this tiny place known all over the world as a downtrodden refugee center some 40 years ago. Today Hong Kong deserves your concern; today Hong Kong needs your vigilance and solidarity; today Hong Kong solicits your prayers.

Glossary

Basic Law *The mini-Constitution of Hong Kong after the transfer of sovereignty on July 1, 1997*

The Basic Law was drafted by a joint committee comprised of 59 Chinese people from Hong Kong (23 members) and the mainland (36 members) who were appointed by the Chinese government. After five years of work, the National People's Congress (NPC) in Beijing voted in April 1990 to approve the final product produced by the committee. The interpretation of the Basic Law as well as amendments to the document can only be done by the Standing Committee of the NPC.

District boards *Elected advisory bodies responsible for making recommendations on such matters as transportation, sanitation and development in relatively small geographical areas of Hong Kong*

Prior to the elections for the 18 district boards in September 1994, some members were appointed by the Hong Kong government and others were elected by the people. Under the political reform proposals of Gov. Chris Patten introduced in October 1992, voters were able to elect all of their district board members for the first time, however. China has stated that those elected in 1994 though will not be able to serve their full four-year term but will have to relinquish their seats upon the change of sovereignty in 1997.

Election Committee *A body composed of 283 district board members*

The Election Committee elected 10 of the 60 members of the Legislative Council (Legco) in the September 1995 polls for the first time. Provisions are specified in the Basic Law for this committee to play a role in the 1999 Legco elections as well.

Executive Council (Exco) *Essentially the cabinet of the Hong Kong government*

The Executive Council is the highest policy making body in the executive-led government of Hong Kong whose 13 to 15 members are appointed by the governor. While executive councilors may offer their own opinions to the governor in their private meetings, Exco operates under a system of confidentiality and collective responsibility, meaning that members are not free to openly discuss the group's deliberations after its meetings nor are they able to publicly express a view that is in opposition to the decision taken by a majority of its members.

Functional constituencies *Segments of the electorate who are primarily divided by job categories, especially professionals and business people*

Each functional constituency has one or two representatives in the Legislative Council (Legco). In the September 1995 election, 30 seats - half of the legislature - were designated for representatives from functional constituencies. However, under Gov. Chris Patten's proposals for political reform that were approved by Legco in June 1994, the electorate for functional constituencies was vastly expanded so that all working people in Hong Kong were able to vote for a functional constituency representative. It was this change that was at the heart of Patten's political reform proposals, proposals that were vehemently opposed by Beijing. Through this system, all working people in Hong Kong could cast two votes for the first time - one for their geographical constituency and one for their functional constituency.

This was an important departure from the past in which the representatives of some functional constituencies were determined by the votes of corporations, not by the individual employees of these companies, and some people did not even have any functional constituency representative at all. Nevertheless, this arrangement still discriminated against those who were not part of the recognized working population - millions of housewives, students and the elderly.

Joint Declaration *An agreement between Britain and China enumerating the principles that will guide the relationship between the governments in Hong Kong and Beijing before and after the change of sovereignty*

Among the important principles enshrined in the Joint Declaration are those that stipulate that Hong Kong and China will relate to each other based on the basis of "one country, two systems," that Hong Kong will enjoy a "high degree of autonomy, except for foreign affairs and defense," that "Hong Kong people will rule Hong Kong." In the Joint Declaration, which was signed in December 1984, Britain and China agreed that Hong Kong's present political and economic systems will remain unchanged for 50 years until the year 2047.

Joint Liaison Group (JLG) *A body composed of representatives from the British and Chinese governments that was established to discuss matters related to Hong Kong's transfer of sovereignty*

The Joint Liaison Group provides an official channel of communication between Hong Kong's present and future sovereign governments to confer and negotiate on issues related to the change of government in the territory in 1997. JLG talks have been held to reach agreements on such practical subjects as the construction of Hong Kong's new airport and new container port facilities, the approval of bilateral civil aviation and trade accords, the extension of existing government licenses or the issuing of new permits and the adoption of hundreds of old laws by the new government - most of which are primarily economic matters.

Legislative Council (Legco) *Hong Kong's legislative body, the highest tier of elected representatives in the community*

Unlike most legislatures in the world whose role it is to initiate and enact laws through an equal balance of power between itself and the other branches of government, the Legislative Council in Hong Kong is severely constrained under the territory's executive-led government, which limits Legco's 60 members to monitoring the policies and programs of the government and approving its budget. Legislative councilors can only initiate their own legislation in the form of private member's bills if they do not have any financial implications for the government. This present relationship between the executive and legislative branches of government will continue after 1997.

Municipal councils *Two bodies whose members are elected by the community to manage its parks and recreational facilities, organize cultural and sporting events, license restaurants and bars and dispose of its garbage, etc.*

Like the district boards above, all 39 members of the Urban Council and 37 members of the Regional Council were directly elected by voters for the first time in the last municipal council elections under British rule, which were held in March 1995. In addition, they share the same fate as the district board members and legislative councilors in that they too will not be able to serve their full four-year terms but will have to vacate their seats when China assumes sovereignty over Hong Kong, even though their functions, like the district boards, are non-political. The municipal councils are distinct from the district boards, however, in that they are responsible for larger geographical areas and have executive powers.

Preliminary Working Committee (PWC) *A body formed by China to assist it with the transition of sovereignty*

Unlike the Preparatory Committee below, the Preliminary Working Committee has no legal standing that is based on either the Joint Declaration or the Basic Law. Formed in July 1993, the committee is composed of 57 members who are about equally divided between Hong Kong and mainland representatives, all of whom are appointed by Beijing. The general thrust of the committee's work can be understood by the areas of responsibility assigned to the five subgroups: education and culture, security, legal matters, constitutional affairs and economic issues. The PWC is seen by many observers in Hong Kong as a body to make recommendations to Beijing to counter the political reform initiatives of Gov. Chris Patten that were introduced less than a year earlier in October 1992. Among the PWC's controversial proposals are those to form a provisional legislature in Hong Kong in 1997 and to dilute the Bill of Rights that was passed in June 1991. Because the committee lacks a legal mandate rooted in any agreements between Britain and China, the Hong Kong government has never cooperated with it. In December 1995, the PWC was disbanded to make way for the Preparatory Committee.

Preparatory Committee *A body composed of Chinese people from Hong Kong and China who are entrusted with the task of making the final arrangements for the transition of sovereignty*

The 150 members of the Preparatory Committee were appointed by Beijing in January 1996. Ninety-four members are from Hong Kong, most of whom are from the business community, indicating China's desire to court good relations with this sector of the community and its willingness to maintain Hong Kong's economic system after 1997. However, China's decision not to include any members of Hong Kong's pro-democracy camp on the committee likewise implies that Beijing hopes to marginalize this group in the future. Among the tasks of the Preparatory Committee are responsibility for forming the Selection Committee, 400 people from Hong Kong who will recommend a person to be the first chief executive of the Special Administrative Region (SAR) government, the highest government official in Hong Kong after 1997 - a decision that must be confirmed by Beijing - and the formation of the provisional legislature. The Preparatory Committee will also act upon the many recommendations made by the Preliminary Working Committee (PWC). In contrast to the PWC, however, the Hong Kong government has recognized the legal status of the Preparatory Committee and has vowed to cooperate with it.

Second stove *A term used to designate an alternative power base in Hong Kong created by the Chinese government*

The "second stove" refers to people in Hong Kong who have been appointed by China to be Hong Kong affairs advisors, district affairs advisors and members of the Preliminary Working Committee (PWC) as well as local citizens who are deputies of the National People's Congress (NPC) in Beijing or members of the Chinese People's Political Consultative Conference (CPPCC) on the mainland. While local residents have been members of the NPC and CPPCC for decades, the strategy of building a second power base to the Hong Kong government that is composed of local people in the territory who hold pro-China views was accelerated in 1992 with the appointment of the first group of Hong Kong affairs advisors and culminated in the creation of the PWC in 1993. By the end of 1994, about 800 people in Hong Kong were members of one or more of these bodies.

Special Administrative Region (SAR) *The political and geographical identity of Hong Kong after its sovereignty has been transferred to China in 1997*

On July 1, 1997, Hong Kong will cease to be a British Crown Colony and will become a Special Administrative Region of the People's Republic of China (PRC), reflecting its political relationship with the central government in Beijing and its geographical affiliation with the rest of the mainland.

Through train *A concept implied in the Joint Declaration and Basic Law that allows those serving the people of Hong Kong under British rule the ability to continue to do so under Chinese sovereignty*

While the "through train" concept applies to senior civil servants and some key members of the judiciary, it is primarily used in reference to Hong Kong's elected representatives, especially its legislative councilors. When talks broke down between China and Britain over Gov. Chris Patten's political reform proposals in December 1993 after 17 rounds of negotiations, Beijing announced that there would no longer be any legislative through train, that all of those elected in the 1994 and 1995 elections could only serve until June 30, 1997 - the end of British rule in Hong Kong. The concept is still valid for the other branches of government, however.

Other Books in the DAGA Press Series

The Militarization of Politics and Society: Southeast Asian Experiences
by Mathews George Chunakara
Published in December 1994

Christianity and Modernization: A Chinese Debate
edited by Philip Wickeri and Lois Cole
Published in May 1995

These books are available by contacting Documentation for Action Groups in Asia (DAGA) at:

CCA Center
96 Second District
Pak Tin Village
Mei Tin Road
Shatin, New Territories
Hong Kong
Telephone: (852) 2697-1917
Fax: (852) 2697-1912
E-mail: daga@asiaonline.net